"This book will save lives. Whether you are
technical diver, this is a must read for anyone in the realm of scuba
diving. Although good training and practical experience are of key
importance, they will never carry you through the next challenge or
emergency you may face: especially underwater.

"For myself, after reading Chapter One of *Staying Alive* (Attitude), I'm
reminded that complacency can often be nurtured by overconfidence.
Good dive planning, including a risk management plan, should never be
overlooked, regardless of the magnitude of the dive or the experience
level of the diver."

Brett B. Hemphill
Director, KARST Underwater Research

"Finally my library is complete. Most divers' libraries – just like mine –
will invariably contain scores of books dedicated to amazing feats,
wonderful destinations, learn to dive this or learn to do that, but very
few deal directly and honestly with the risks associated with
participating in this wonderful sport.

"Not only is *Staying Alive* incredibly informative, but Steve reveals that
the process of mitigating risk is not tedious and dull: it can in fact be a
lot of fun.

"This book is a must for any recreational or technical diver who takes
diving seriously and has the desire to come home after every dive."

Paul V. Toomer
Director of Technical Training
Scuba Schools International

"*Staying Alive* ought to be an essential part of every diving instructor's
tool kit. There is risk in everything we do; what we do for work, and
what we do for play. You cannot avoid risk, you just need to manage it.
The latest book from Steve Lewis will help to get you pointed in the
right direction."

Rosemary E Lunn
Diving Journalist and Industry Analyst

Staying Alive:

Risk Management Techniques for Advanced Scuba Diving

Steve Lewis

Published by SL Publications,

A Division of Techdiver Publishing & Training,
11 White Birch Drive, Rosseau, ON Canada P0C 1J0
eMail: slpub@techdivertraining.org

Front cover photo of the author at Jackson Blue Spring by Michael Robertson.
© M. Robertson 2013

Printed by CreateSpace, An Amazon.com Company

Cover design by: Surf Ad & Design Co.
This book is set in Garamond and Calibri

ISBN: 978-0-9812280-4-4

Staying Alive:
Risk Management Techniques for Advanced Scuba Diving

By Steve Lewis

"I don't want to write about diving; I don't want to talk about diving; I don't want to photograph people diving; I don't want to think about people diving; all I want to do is **GO** diving. And when I do it, I wanna make damn sure I don't die in the process!"

Wayland Rhys-Morgan *(friend of the author)*

FIRST EDITION
January 2014

Techdiver Publishing & Training
11 White Birch Drive, Rosseau, ON Canada P0C 1J0

DISCLAIMER

Advanced diving is a potentially hazardous practice that exposes divers to considerable risk including death if executed incorrectly or without appropriate planning and procedures in place. Even with specialized training, equipment and experience, these risks do not disappear, but are always present and ready to grab the ill-prepared and foolhardy. This book is not intended as a substitute for training, equipment or as an open invitation to any certified and experienced diver to abandon common sense in pursuit of activities beyond the scope of his or her abilities.

The contents of this book represent the author's views on various aspects of risk management for advanced diving. However, the reader should understand and be warned that the procedures mentioned in this book are not necessarily proven nor are they sanctioned in part or as a whole by any accredited scuba certifying body. Some aspects of the risk management methods presented here may be disproved or displaced as new information is unearthed. The reader is strongly advised to keep up-to-date on new developments and studies in these fields as they are released.

Neither the author nor publisher accepts responsibility for the accuracy of examples or interpolations of any decompression algorithm, published limit or associated table included in this work. While care and skill have been employed in the preparation and writing of this book, the reader should be aware of these limitations.

DEDICATION

To Edd Sorenson, Superman. An inspiration to all of us. I just hope, buddy, that when the next punter ignores the guidelines and gets his or her butt stuck underwater someplace dark and nasty, you are around to fish 'em out.

NOTE ABOUT UNITS OF MEASUREMENT USED IN THIS BOOK:

Throughout this book measurements for mass, distance, volume and temperature, use primarily the International System of Units and their derivatives. These are referred to interchangeably in this text as SI units or the metric system. I believe many of the calculations required for all types of dive are much simpler when the metric system is employed. However, wherever practical, 'imperial equivalents' have been supplied for those still working in U.S. customary units. Please be aware that the equivalent measurements given are rarely exact conversions, but are in line with common use and similar to those found in general diving texts; for example, 10 kilograms = 22 pounds; 40 metres / 130 feet; 14 litres or 0.5 cubic feet, rather than the more accurate but somewhat pedantic 10 kilograms = 22.05 pounds, 40 metres / 131.23 feet, and 14 litres or 0.49 cubic feet. This practice results in some minor discrepancies in examples given in the text, but nothing like the discrepancies resulting from the diving community's widespread use of un-calibrated measuring devices.

In cases where imperial measurements are uncommon – in rebreather diving for example – only metric units are used.

CONTENTS

ACKNOWLEDGEMENTS

Although it sounds a little corny, it is absolutely true to say that without the help of a lot of folks this book would never have happened or would have taken a very different form. That list of helpers, mentors and supporters is long; but I did not keep notes. Instead, I am going to circle the wagons and mention only those who contributed ideas, suggestions and support during the past few months while this book was being put together. I hope that those who recognize their longer-term contributions – apparent in the methods I use to teach, and my overall approach to risk management – will forgive my omissions.

I was in fact working on another project when a long-time friend and colleague pointed out to me that this book, or at least a book for divers about risk management, would be a good next move. Because of him, the last three or four months have been hectic, but fun. I would like to thank Chris Richardson for the idea and encouragement to get this book written and published within a very short timeframe.

I also have to single out the following friends and dive buddies. Firstly, Gareth Lock for taking a look at the working draft, making suggestions and putting together the foreword. However, thanks directed at Gareth have to include more. While he is an excellent technical diver and photographer, it's his career in the Royal Air Force as both a 'Flying Supervisor' and a 'Tactical Flight Instructor,' that is particularly germane to the topic of risk management. What sets Gareth apart in our community is that he has applied 'Human Factors' techniques from his military aviation background in a spirited endeavor to draw attention to how dive accidents happen; and from that point of greater understanding, what can be done to improve diver safety. Check out his Diving Incident and Safety Resource Centre website at www.disrc.com.

Paul Vincent Toomer is Director of Technical Training for Scuba Schools International and he was one of the book's early reviewers. I have been mates with Paul for a good while and have great respect for his commitment to continuing diver education, and diver safety. Joining him in the review task was Brett Hemphill. Brett is one of those low-key explorer types who disappears for a couple of weeks every now and then to work on the most gob-smacking expeditions. He has yet to land a TV reality show, but who knows what the future holds.

Mark Powell is internationally known as an active technical diving instructor and author. His *Deco for Divers* remains one of the most influential and useful books for advanced divers. I am grateful to him for helping to review this book at very short notice. Mark, you can be a hard guy to track down: thanks a bunch.

Big Mike, Michael Arthur Robertson, took the picture used on the cover. Thanks to him for that, and thanks also for being the best-humored dive-buddy I know. He even drinks the correct type of Scotch: from the right island, although not from the appropriate distillery. Thanks too for Kevin L. Jones, Greg Regnier, Jim Clark, and Michael Menduno. The four of them sense-checked and proofed, prodded and poked my original manuscript.

Along the way, owners and senior staff at several "dive companies" have helped too. Their assistance has ranged from supplying a photograph, to loaning me gear… some of which was tested to destruction. In those cases, they had the grace not to ask too many questions. In no specific order, these companies and individuals include: American Underwater Products, and in particular Nick Hollis and Dave Burroughs at Hollis; Pete Nawrocky at Dive Rite; Sean Webb and Marcus Darler at O'Three Drysuits; Martin Parker and Nicky Finn at AP Diving; Mike Fowler at Silent Diving; Bobby Franklin at Underwater Light Dude; Chris Richardson at HOG/Edge gear; Corey Mearns at Light Monkey; Rosemary (Roz) Lunn at Underwater Marketing Company; Jill Heinerth and Robert McCellan at Heinerth Productions; David Concannon at Explorer Consulting; Stacy Martin, John Weston and all the crew at Cave Adventurers; Pete Murray, the big fish at ScubaBoard; and dive buddies not already mentioned above: Kenny Paramore and Erik Van Dorn. There are more. Apologies to those I missed.

The best until last of course: Leah Leslie, without whom none of this would be possible, and who has been with me for most of this crazy, and exhilarating ride.

FOREWORD

Whilst it might appear to be clichéd and lazy to start a foreword with the closing remarks of the author's previous work, I believe the closing words from Steve's last book are very apt here.

"... The more challenging the dive and the greater the distance between it and mainstream sport-diving limits, the more risk is involved. No amount of training, experience, equipment or good luck will completely mitigate the risk. We would do well to remind ourselves often that, if we participate in technical diving, there is always a risk of serious injury or death."

Diving can be risky, irrespective of the level of diving we undertake. However, something that is commonly done by all divers, even if only subconsciously, is to try to determine the level of risk, whether anything can be done about it and, as a consequence, whether the benefit is personally worth the real or perceived risk.

Traditionally risk is defined as a combination of the probability and the impact of an event materializing. Unfortunately, as humans we are not very good at determining likelihood for a whole variety of psychological reasons, not least because our perception and acceptance of risk changes as we undertake more of the activity and gain more skills, knowledge and experience. If you look through magazines, forums and blogs, there are a significant number of examples where divers chose to ignore the likelihood of the event happening: an event that ended up in a minor injury, or worse, a fatality. The work I have been doing over the last few years has been to try to create a culture where we can discuss incidents and their causes in a manner which allows lessons to be learned. For this reason I was very pleased when Steve asked me to write this foreword.

Education and experience are two of the best ways of mitigating any risk and Steve's book provides a number of examples of how risks can be dealt with. These range from decompression and gas consumption planning, to exposure mitigation, to checklist and pre-dive processes, to debriefing the dives themselves. All this so lessons can be learned. Each section deals with a different subject, with real and credible scenarios provided, which exemplify the way in which the issues can be identified and the risks mitigated. This approach provides a refreshing look into a subject which is lacking in the majority of agency training materials; and therefore anyone who dives is likely to learn something from this book.

Whilst training organizations and peers try to prepare us for the time when risk becomes an issue, we need to recognize that we need to be personally responsible for the activities we undertake. Regrettably there is no benefit in having 20:20 hindsight if we don't apply it to foresight when we plan future activities. Learn from your mistakes, better still, learn from someone else's, thereby making your own diving safer.

Diving should be fun and whilst we cannot remove all the risks in scuba because of the physical and technical environment we are in, we can certainly reduce the likelihood of them occurring by being aware of the risks and mitigating them. One of those mitigations is not to go diving; there is nothing worth dying for on a dive.

Gareth Lock MSc.
Founder, Cognitas Incident Research and Management Ltd

AUTHOR'S NOTE: Why write this

"… Still a man hears what he wants to hear: and disregards the rest"

The Boxer 1968, Paul Simon

Everyone who sets out to write a book has some specific goal in mind; something that makes the project worth the effort; a reason to do it. That reason might be to tell a story, to educate, amuse, express an opinion, or simply to share a talent with the world. Mine is to stop people unintentionally killing themselves. This is, as my editor tells me, my palpable polemic: an association I am happy to live with.

As well, when writers start to work on their books, they will often have a reasonably good idea who is going to buy and read them… especially authors of "How-To" and "Self-Help" books such as this one. I had in mind recreational divers like you: all types of recreational divers. Open-circuit, closed-circuit, technical, advanced, newly-certified divers, old experienced divers, sport divers, underwater photographers, cold-water wreck divers, cave divers, sidemount divers, and everything in between.

Post-dive surveys tell us that we each get something unique from our diving, and many of us prefer one or two "types" of diving over all others. However, regardless of which pigeon-hole we slot ourselves into, all recreational divers have two things in common. The first is that we dive for fun. It's not our work: we rather see it as a remedy for work. The second is that diving can be a dodgy way to get one's kicks, and if things go wonky when we're in the water we can die, seriously hurt ourselves, or worse, do irreparable damage to our body and exist for decades immobile and comatose. Frighteningly, we do not even have to be underwater to be at risk. People have died while floating on the surface!

Welcome to real recreational scuba rather than the whitewashed version sold by the marketing department of Quik-and-Dirty Scuba Training. If you have been told that scuba diving is safe, someone has lied to you. Make no mistake, diving in every one of its many forms and in any type of water – even a swimming pool – is fundamentally treacherous and alarmingly quick to harm.

When I published *The Six Skills and Other Discussions*, the plan was to help divers understand some of the things that have allowed me enjoy technical diving for the past 20-plus years. In that book, emphasis was placed on the mental skills that most dive books – even technical dive books – seem to ignore, or at best, alight on with only the lightest of possible touches. My goal with that book was to get people thinking creatively about their approach to diving, to dive planning and to execution. And perhaps through that exercise, to make them better divers. The goal here is more direct. Too many people are dying to continue ignoring what's going on in our community. Something needs fixing. Something is broken.

Success in diving, indeed any form of high-risk endeavor, is really about risk management. Good, enjoyable diving is exciting, but the threats associated with diving have to be managed and maintained at an acceptable level.

Beyond the world of diving, risk managers use a tool called Composite Risk Index. It works something like this. The Impact of Risk is assessed on a Likert Scale: 1 to 5, where 1 represents the minimum possible impact, numbers 2, 3, and 4 build towards 5, which signifies the maximum. Usually Composite Risk Index is used to understand and quantify the impact of a business or marketing process. A level-5 impact would tend to indicate some sort of business failure and not death as it would in diving.

The Probability of Occurrence is assessed on a similar scale with 1 representing a very low probability that something bad will happen while 5 represents a very high probability of it happening… essentially that the event in question is inevitable.

The Composite Risk Index (which equals the Impact of Risk multiplied by its Probability of Occurrence) will thus present values ranging from 1 through 25. This range is usually arbitrarily divided into three sub-ranges: Low 1-8; Medium 9-16; or High 17-25.

In activities such as diving, it is unusual to apply the metrics of something as structured as the Composite Risk Index. To begin with, the probability of dangerous episode is difficult to estimate, since the past data on frequencies are not readily available, and probability does not imply certainty at any point.

Also, the Impact of Risk in diving is difficult to quantify, since the probable outcome of many occurrences results sooner or later in death by drowning: there simply are not that many ones in scuba but there are a whole bunch of fives.

Therefore the approach of most divers to risk, is somewhat different and much simpler. Risk is assessed primarily and quite simply on its likelihood of occurrence. Divers put in place a system designed to avoid or mitigate the possibilities of injury. Training, experience, the development and adoption of best practices, community pressure, equipment, and so on are all parts of that system. If the system is thought to provide an "acceptable" degree of reliability, and the diver thinks him or herself familiar with and fluent with the workings of that system, the risk itself is said to be acceptable.

Oddly enough, the system is misleadingly complex and to be fluent requires a degree of understanding not commonly taught to recreational divers. You might be forgiven for suggesting that our perception of the system's reliability floats on a platform cobbled together from good fortune; and ignorance.

Yet another approach, and one all of us should be aware of, makes an assessment of risk based on the magnitude of regret should the type of event being assessed actually happen. Individuals who adopt this method of risk analysis are most often unwilling to accept the hazards associated with diving no matter how unlikely the event. These folks do not become divers.

This last approach to risk is safe, all the others are not!

And so, we arrive at the 'Edict of Liability and Responsibility,' which divers, certainly technical divers, must accept. No form of diving is safe; and in real terms, no high-stress, high-risk, fun activity is ever safe. However, this does not mean divers need to be cavalier about personal safety or off-hand when it comes to their continued well-being. Quite the opposite; the vast majority of experienced technical divers are risk averse. They use any and every tool they can to help them identify, assess, avoid and mitigate the menace inherent in poking one's head underwater and breathing compressed gas.

Managing the perils of diving is a fluid process that starts with risk identification and classification, and aims to arrive at a spot where risks that cannot be reduced or avoided altogether can at least be softened or shared. Compared to the long to-do list that a diver has to check through before they can dive "safely," risk management is a blindingly simple process, and it works: almost 100 percent of the time. True accidents are rare. More importantly, over the past 20-odd years, as more advanced, deeper, longer dives have become the new norm, risk management too has evolved a broadened and much longer list of suggested best practices. Divers can apply these to planning and execution, and by so doing be proactive in the worthwhile fight to keep themselves safe… or safer.

The end result is that although diving carries risk, managing those risks is much more straightforward than it was a generation ago.

Sadly, some dive "accidents" are not accidents at all but the result of deviating from the risk-management process or neglecting it all-together. Let me rephrase that to say **most** diving accidents are not accidents at all. They are, at best, the outcome of some misadventure, sometimes the result of an avoidable mistake or oversight, and at worst the result of arrogance and hubris.

The key question we, the survivors, might ask each other is: Why do people do that? Why ignore well-established, sound principles, and snub best practice: why wing it?

There are many possible answers, but the one that's obvious to me is lack of understanding. Either people have not been told about the dangers associated with diving, or they know what they are but do not believe that IT – an accident resulting in serious injury or death – could happen to them. Perhaps too, they understand the risks fully but do not have the means to change their behavior, when often a modest change is all that's required for them to dive under the protection of a decent risk-management plan. They might easily enjoy a cushion of safety, but misunderstand how little effort is required to put that cushion under their rump should they slip and fall.

If you look around at the huge catalog of diving books, you may notice that very few put the process of risk management under a favorable and revealing light. Few if any paint it as fun: which I believe it can be. Risk management is not a chore, but it is critically important; and in the next few pages, my hope is that Paul Simon was wrong and I can convince you to agree with me!

Thanks

Steve Lewis
Muskoka, Ontario: Marianna/Orlando, Florida: September 2013 – January 2014

Chapter One

ATTITUDE: It all starts right here with you...

Many years ago, a mathematics teacher and cave explorer named Sheck Exley drew up a five-item shortlist of reasons to explain why divers were dying in caves. His list became the foundation of common best practice for a generation of cave divers, and although specifically aimed at the cave diving community, was used for many years as the underpinning of accident analysis taught to all budding technical divers.

Exley's five principles of 'safe' cave diving – published in his book, Basic Cave Diving: A Blueprint for Survival – were Training, Guideline, Gas, Depth, and Lights. (Giving rise to the mnemonic Thank God Good Divers Live.) These were expanded for general technical diving use to: Never exceed your training and experience; Always know your position relative to a safe exit/place to surface; Plan gas volume needs including ample gas for contingencies; Choose the best gas for the target depth and duration; Be correctly equipped for the planned dive, and be familiar with and practiced in the use of every piece of equipment your team will be carrying.

Sometime after the publication of Exley's original work, as the popularity of and market for technical diving grew beyond the expectations of those early tech pioneers, later amendments expanded his "guidelines for safety" to cover eight categories. Known as survival techniques these were: Attitude; Knowledge; Training; Gas Supply; Gas Mix; Exposure; Equipment; and Operations.

These eight categories form the backbone of this book. Each element can be interpreted for modern-day diving and employed to make your diving more enjoyable, more rewarding, and safer, regardless of whether it's your intention to dive in a cave, do a technical dive of some other type, or whether the ink on your open-water certification card is still wet. The hope is that you are looking for information to become a better diver.

So, we begin with Attitude because safe diving begins with the right attitude: one that understands and gives priority to safety.

ACCIDENT ANALYSIS: The influence of Attitude

We hope to learn from the mistakes of others in order to avoid paying the price of making those same mistakes ourselves. This is the principle behind accident analysis. However, reading about a dive "accident" and teasing out its lessons can be tough.

The task of decoding and cataloguing the specifics of events that led up to the kind of diving misadventure that results in injury or death usually involves a mix of forensic and contingent analysis on the diver's gear, and some type of functional analysis of the reasons, purpose and motivation behind the diver's behavior.

A detailed examination of the equipment used, analyzing how that equipment performed during the dive, and examining what gases were used, all present singular and exceptional challenges to those charged with asking questions after an incident. But as problematic as those tasks may be, they are effortless compared to the job of finding out WHY somebody did what they did. To discover that, we move into a largely grey kingdom ruled over by assumption and speculation. This is especially true when the person at the center of events is no longer available to tell us what made him (and occasionally her) do the things he did.

So how can we best discover exactly what it was that caused the house of cards to fall over; and how things got to a point where someone had the scare of their life,
injured themselves, or died?

In some cases, a diver may have been aware there was a heightened level of threat, but was bullied by someone into doing the dive anyway. Can we place any blame on a diver who finds himself in this situation? I vote to say, No! You may feel differently, but in these special cases, if there's blame to be had, it seems unfair to lay it at the feet of the victim. In our final analysis, we can correctly say that this person may have been scared, hurt or killed because of poor attitude, but not their own poor attitude.

In some other instances, we can make a safe assumption that the victim simply did not know enough to recognize that they were taking an unholy risk. With apologies to any students of Catholic Doctrine in the audience, let's call this a sin of omission. The diver's attitude "allowed" them to undertake a dive without knowing the special risks it involved. On a scale of culpability, perhaps we can apportion less blame to a diver guilty of omission than those who fall into our next category: sins of commission.

In these cases, a diver appears to have had full awareness that what they planned to do was totally the opposite of what's recommended. They worked under some illusion that even though they were taught the correct way, that was not the right way for them to do it. Perhaps they felt special, gifted, untouchable, lucky.

When someone has full knowledge that their actions are outside normal best practice – diving in a cave without cave training, conducting decompression dives with only the knowledge gained from internet chat groups – they may pull it off time and time again. They may develop a strong feeling that since they got away with it once, they will get away with it again.

This "Normalization of Deviance" is perhaps the worst fallout from a completely wrong attitude because, diving in a cave and decompression diving are 'easy'… until something goes wrong and then people get hurt.

With these cases, the lessons to be learned are clear and there's little ambiguity, but often, it's hard for some of us to accept that with sins of commission, fault does fall at the diver's feet. This is a harsh truth. Observers wishing to remain neutral and politically correct may seek to obscure it, but it remains the most logical answer to any nagging questions asking what happened. What happened is largely or wholly that the victim's luck ran out, as happens with most gambles sooner or later.

Even surviving dive buddies can throw an investigation for a loop by glossing over perceived mistakes his/her buddy (now a victim) made during the prep for the dive or the dive itself, in the hope of preserving that person's reputation as a "safe diver."

One of the classics pointed out to me by a friend who has investigated several incidents involving divers on rebreathers is the: "He always used a checklist" syndrome.

During the past couple of years – certainly since the proceedings of Rebreather Forum 3.0 were made public – there has been a community-wide outcry trying to convince rebreather divers to use a physical "paper" checklist to keep track of the complex steps in the correct assembly and pre-dive preparations for their rebreather unit.

Such lists are strongly recommended even on models such as AP Diving's Evolution and Inspiration, which both prompt users to scroll through an on-screen checklist when the unit is turned on.

During post-incident investigations my friend – a US-based lawyer – has noted in the last few cases that dive buddies swear they witnessed the victim using a checklist pre-dive. "This after several years of finding no signs of checklists during investigations in 100 percent of more than two dozen cases I have been called to evaluate," he explained.

So, can we interpret this to indicate a sudden community-wide chance of behavior? Has the use of checklists become the new norm, and, since dive buddies of several victims insist they were used before the fateful dive, does it turn out that their use has not saved CCR divers from making errors?

"Not really," says my friend. "Because when we push it and ask the "witness" what the list looked like, was it a laminated card, a page in a notebook, a sheet pasted inside their rebreather, they recant. We commonly hear: "Well… he always used one but I guess he forgot it on this dive." Point made! The tightrope walker always used a safety net except the time he fell to his death.

For the sake of our analysis, we can see that this is not an example of someone being bullied into a dive or being ignorant of the risks they were exposing themselves to. This indicates the worst attitudinal problem for any diver: Complacency.

COMPLACENCY KILLS

Human nature being what it is, complacency is part of almost everyone's makeup. A higher level of experience and even professional-level qualifications do not guarantee that a diver will make the right decisions and take appropriate action before his dive should a piece of kit not be perfectly correct or check out as 100 percent functional.

Chances are that most of you have seen a diver go ahead and make a dive with something as "unimportant" as a fin or mask strap that's a little dodgy; ignoring the fact that being able to swim and read one's gauges is important! This may be a smaller issue on a dive to 10 metres in warm water with mild surface conditions, but it shows a certainly level of complacency and poor attitude towards how best to avoid potential problems.

The real difficulty is that complacency is an easy mind-set to fall into. It can be a function of ignorance but more usually is the result of over-confidence. Certainly, the confidence that naturally comes from experience is a potential issue. The more experience one gains in ANY field, the more likely one is to fall into a complacent frame of mind. I sometimes catch myself making inappropriate decisions when I am diving alone and have to be on guard against this failing all the time, especially when I do not have students to look after.

And speaking of students (and diving with buddies who have less experience), I have had to remind myself on more than a few occasions to counter their potential complacency towards me. I make a point of briefing these folks to remind them that I can experience difficulties in the water. It's never happened with students, and although on a couple of occasions, I've needed buddies to help pull me out of a scrape, the day may very well come when I may need full-on assistance. It may never happen – I hope it never happens – but I don't want anyone to get complacent when I'm their dive buddy. Complacency kills experienced divers… especially when they believe themselves or their more experienced buddy to be infallible.

Sadly, the inter-relationship between over-confidence, complacency and a dangerous attitude is abundantly illustrated by an alarmingly long list of dive incidents where the primary – and often only – causal event, the thing that started a sickeningly inevitable chain reaction resulting in a diver's death, is the "it can't happen to me" attitude.

These examples range from ignoring the suggestion from another team member that a cylinder labelled oxygen be analyzed before being used at depths approaching 27 metres / 80 feet, to a closed-circuit rebreather diver using oxygen sensors that he knew where out of date and potentially current limited.

In both these cases – as well as many others – the victims had ample training and experience to conduct the dives they had planned. They were suitably equipped, and had full knowledge of the community's accepted best practices and what should be done. They chose to ignore all that and, as with several CCR divers who elected not to use a checklist "today", they did not come back from their dive.

To learn from their mistakes, we have to ask why they did what they did. The only helpful answer is complacency; as speculative as this may sound. They got into trouble because they did not think the rules applied to them. That attitude is wrong, and they found out the hard way that the rules apply to us all regardless of our self-confidence, experience and level of certification.

Complacency is basic human nature, and in our everyday life, after doing something repetitively, many of us start to cut corners. We don't bother taking a couple of minutes to analyze a gas we are "sure" came from banked nitrox, we don't swap out a fuel cell (oxygen sensor) that's past its best-before date for that "simple dive," we don't worry about "wet breathing" a deco regulator before beginning our dive because it worked yesterday. We know how something is supposed to be done, but it's "too much trouble or not worth the bother," so we take the shorter route: we become complacent. What makes complacency habit forming is that some people get away with it time after time after time.

SELF-ASSESSMENT: An Antidote for complacency
Cleaning out a bunch of old files and student records recently, I found a copy of my

original dive-plan template – something my buddies and I used for several years when we first started to do deep mix dives – and I was reminded why we scrapped it and drew up a new one: It's missing an important element.

If memory serves, the error was pointed out by Bret Gilliam. At that time, Bret was president of Technical Diving International (TDI) and he was gathering information for student manuals and asking instructors to contribute things like teaching notes, learning goals, and so on. Among the various bits and pieces I contributed was a spreadsheet template of the dive plan my buddies and I were using, and that I was also teaching students to use.

"It's good but you're missing something…" he told me after looking it over for a few minutes. "Something critical."

I checked it a couple more times and to my eyes the plan looked pretty comprehensive and exhaustive. I told him I could not see what was wrong with it.

"There's nothing in it about conducting any level of self-assessment before you jump into the water," he said.
"Don't you think that's worthy of a line or two?"

Checklists and complete dive plans are intended as a good first-line of defence against diver complacency. They help to counter oversight and swing attention back to things that it's easy for divers, even very experienced ones, to take for granted. We can all probably come up with a long list of things that, without a checklist, it's possible, even easy, to overlook. A checklist and a detailed dive plan, discussed and agreed on with every member of the dive team, is a great way to start a safe dive.

But, as Gilliam pointed out to me in his office in a refurbished textile mill in a trendy little town in Maine back in 1997, the most complete, comprehensive and meticulous dive plan cannot prevent things going horribly wrong if the folks executing it aren't as present, correct and as ready as their equipment is to do the dive.

Self-assessment is now included in the pre-dive checks for several tech agency courses, but like the requirement to analyze and mark EVERY bottle of gas, to check rebreather fuel cells for performance, or to pre-breathe EVERY regulator – or any of the other listed items on a checklist or dive plan – it is entirely self-policed, and quickly becomes worthless if any one member of a dive team shortcuts that "policing operation."

The self-assessment process is simple enough. You ask yourself a couple of easy-to-answer questions and answer them honestly. Better yet, when the dive leader has completed her own self-assessment, she might want to check with everyone on the team to make sure they all "passed" the self-assessment check too.

Don't forget that the technical diver's credo: "Any diver can call any dive for any reason…" also includes "at any time" and that covers thumbing a dive before anyone gets wet. Far better to be on the surface thinking: "I wish I were diving," than being on a dive wishing you were back on the surface.

When we dive – even on those dives that seem like a simple bimble around in shallow water – we must ask ourselves if our plans account for any and all hazards. For our purposes, a hazard in the case of diving is any agent or situation posing a credible level of threat to our life, health and property, those of any team member, or the environment in which we intend to dive.

When we make a proper and realistic self-assessment, that assessed risk includes things that are not visible or readily apparent to our buddies. First and foremost is our personal level of comfort.

To check this is in fact the case and that our planned dive is within our comfort-zone, we ask ourselves: Considering ALL the perils associated with the dive as planned, do we find them acceptable? Does the plan cope with things and events that have some significant probability of occurrence during that dive? Circumstances may change at any time. Nobody can predict precisely when and how things may go pear-shaped because so much depends on circumstances that may not be at all predicable. We have to ask ourselves if our plan makes allowance for this and if not, why not. Are we comfortable if it does not?

Recreational divers, even those engaged in serious technical dives, are under no contract and are not protected by legislation. Each of us is responsible for our safety and well-being, and – to some extent through enlightened self-interest and the tenets of friendship – with that of our buddies. Honest answers to these questions will help keep us safe and should be asked before every dive; no matter how simple and inconsequential the dive seems.

In addition, there are several other questions we might ask ourselves as part of the "self-assessment" process that should be carried out long before we pull on a drysuit. They concern personal health. We need to ask if we are comfortable with our personal condition. Are we free from dehydration and fatigue? Is our cardio and general physical fitness up to the stress of the dive as planned? Do we have angina, epilepsy, diabetes, asthma, and if so is it controlled enough to dive for fun? Do we have adequate strength to do the dive as planned? Have we learned and practiced the critical safety skills required on this dive as planned? Are we diving drunk, are we hung-over or stoned?

Are we physically and mentally ready to do the dive as planned and if something hits a fan while we are down there, are we ready to deal with it appropriately?

This seems like a suitable time to draw attention to concept that suggests unskilled individuals (new divers for example), rate their ability to do a task (conduct a complex dive for instance) far above their competence. In classic examples of "they do not know what they do not know" a series of experiments conducted by two members of the psychology department at Cornell University, David Dunning and Justin Kruger, proposed that, for a given learned task, incompetent people overestimate their own level of skill; fail to recognize genuine skill in others; fail to recognize the extremity of their inadequacy.

This so-called Dunning–Kruger effect may only apply to individuals with a bias resulting from certain cultural backgrounds – privileged Americans in the original studies, but what later observers have called the narcissistic 'selfie photo-taking' generation – however, it's certainly worth a sidebar mention in any serious attempt at realistic self-assessment.

It may seem a little odd, but during self-assessment one should also ask: Do I believe in my buddy's abilities, and do I feel they have the skills and experience required to do the dive as planned? Are we being over-confident expecting ourselves and each member of the team to do the dive as planned? Does that hold up if we become separated? Do I feel the same should it become necessary to rescue a buddy on this dive... can I rescue them and can they rescue me?

Self-assessment does not always return a positive answer. But self-assessment is a positive habit to develop and it needs to become part of the pre-dive preparations for EVERY dive: especially any dive that requires the use of decompression gases to manage a decompression obligation, or that takes place in a hard overhead environment.

IT REALLY IS ALL ON YOUR SHOULDERS

Perhaps my attitude is colored by many years of working with students who are progressing through technical diving programs, but I do not believe there is anything particularly unusual about a diver feeling apprehensive about a pinnacle dive. A certain level of nervousness, a slight concern because this is the "biggest" or deepest or longest dive is normal and to be expected. However, if the weight of those misgivings is heavier than the satisfaction one expects from the dive, call it off. Wrecks, caves, reefs, big fish etc. will all be there waiting for the next attempt... and the one after that.

A good buddy will support you and your decision to bail on a dive. A good diver is empathetic and works hard to cultivate a good attitude towards personal safety and the safety of others. A good attitude is sound logic based on enlightened self-interest. When all is said and done, which is better for you: a buddy who is a hair's breadth from falling apart like a cheap suit because you bullied them into diving with you, or someone who's happy to be diving with you and who shared the responsibility of planning and executing the dive? Simply put, we cannot expect help and support from a diver who is uncomfortable, near panic and ready to bail themselves.

In the final analysis, only you can tell if you are ready to dive. Only you know if your confidence is founded on experience, understanding and capability. Only you know if you have practiced the basic skills and the specific skills you may need if things go wonky on this next dive.

Our friends and the folks we respect and hold as role models or mentors may be able to alter our outlook or change our attitude, but nobody can do it faster and more effectively than we can ourselves. So, if our goal is to become a safer diver, surely the best place to start is to take a close and critical look at our own attitude and poke around in there to be sure that any holes or threadbare spots are too small to let bad stuff seep in.

We are all very capable of normalizing our personal deviance. The more experience we gain, the more vulnerable we become. We are all guilty of some violation of recognized standards of practice. Most of us walk away from that violation and it goes almost unnoticed. The tricky part is that if we get away with something once, there is a temptation to become a repeat offender. Human nature, ego, laziness all conspire to make it so. Over time, even egregious violations may become normalized.

You may have witnessed this happening in yourself, to a buddy or a co-worker.

A couple of months back, I was listening to a skilled craftsman explaining the set-up of a rather complex wood saw to an apprentice. Partway through he explained that although the tool's user manual "and probably your classroom book" suggested a very specific approach, he'd learned that it was quicker and just as efficient to ignore that and do things a completely different way.

I don't know enough about industrial machinery to know if his suggestion to the new guy was flagrantly dangerous, but I recognize normalized deviance when I see it.

Deviations from accepted practice can persist for years before the genuine risks they invoke one day manifest themselves in the form of a serious "accident." This is an attitudinal problem.

So at this point, the question you should be asking yourself is not: Am I giving my buddies a snow job, but rather: Am I lying to myself?

Chapter Two

KNOWLEDGE/WISDOM: safe diving through insight

I am unsure what definitions for wisdom and knowledge we'd find if we looked them up in the Oxford English Dictionary or Webster's, but I am quite sure that in the context of risk management for diving we can say that **Knowledge** is understanding how something works, while **Wisdom** is understanding how that knowledge applies to the specifics of safe diving.

If we needed to come up with an alternative, we could also say that knowledge is something we gain through a process of learning – facts, truths, experience and data – and wisdom is making consistently good decisions based on the things that we've learned (i.e. knowledge).

Or, perhaps more germane to our present topic, we might say that knowing something doesn't mean one automatically avoids being bitten in the backside by the lessons it has to teach.

At the beginning of the previous chapter, I mentioned the primary reason for writing this book. The most important, the special ingredient in a way, is a desire to share a little wisdom with readers. To offer aegis to those willing to accept it and share the voyage of self-discovery that usually follows getting the metaphorical "slap on the side of your head." In a formal classroom/practical program, this is the primary goal.

Every day an instructor works with his or her students, it is wisdom he or she aims to share. I'm not suggesting that every instructor starts the day thinking: "The wisdom for today will be…" and consciously then goes about imparting that particular piece of wisdom to his or her charges. Few of us, few instructors, think that way. The process is more subtle, more implied than that, but this is essentially what happens when a decent professional runs a decent diver education program.

And in the context of teaching a scuba program, imparting wisdom through knowledge should not be just a remotely possible outcome. The dynamics of debate and discussion being what they are, it is relatively simple for an instructor to light a little flame of insight in the folks they're working with: to leave behind a faint sillage of curiosity and inquisitiveness that goes far beyond what's written in the textbook. In a book the effect is not so easy to reproduce.

Certainly in a single chapter, a few thousand words with a couple of graphs and pictures thrown in, it is close to impossible. So, my hope is that this whole book will leave readers a little wiser, and if possible, able to attach their own brand of wisdom to any knowledge they may gain from reading it.

KNOWLEDGE

This chapter is about knowledge and wisdom, so let's walk through a technique that might be employed in a "decent" scuba program to turn the first into the second. Let's use the example of Boyle's Law since most divers are familiar with it and certainly ran across it during formal classroom presentations from open-water diver training on up the scuba educational tree/bush/scrub.

It's the gas law that explains why balloons getting bigger as they float from depth to the surface. Never seen a balloon on a dive – aside from a lift bag or DSMB – but Boyle's is the reason divers know not to hold their breath; and it's the primary reason why a specific volume of gas will last a diver less time at depth than it does on the surface.

That is knowledge, but it is knowledge without wisdom. There is more to be had from Mr. Boyle. Boyle's law states that at constant temperature for a fixed mass, the absolute pressure and volume of a gas are inversely proportional.

There are other ways to express it, but that's the way most textbooks present it to diving students. I believe most divers consider Boyle's Law to be about this and little else.

Diving textbooks don't bother to share much more detail with "average" Joe and Jill divers so this is not surprising.

Even the average divemaster candidate potentially going on the become an open-water instructor will learn that definition, memorize it word for word and may be able to quote it verbatim or point it out in a police lineup, but the chances are good that he or she will never be encouraged to investigate its ramifications any further.

Let's go a little further right now. Taking our notion that wisdom is the singular result of taking learned facts one additional step, we can shock and surprise if we state that Boyle's Law is not scientifically accurate when gas is at high pressures – the sort of pressures we'd expect to find in a scuba cylinder.

When he was gathering data and drawing up his gas law, Boyle – recognised outside diving circles as the first modern chemist – worked within the confines of 17th century technology. He was safe to assume gases behave as ideal gases because compressors capable of squishing air or other gases to several hundred times atmospheric pressure were unheard of.

His assumption, fine for day-to-day operations in the late 1600s, we know today is incorrect. Gases have mass and interact with their surroundings. Consequently, gas at pressure is anything but ideal. Real gas, all gases – and certainly the "diving" gases, oxygen, nitrogen and helium – exhibit slightly different behavior when put under great pressure, and each has a different compressibility.

All well and good, but you may ask, what difference does that make to us as divers? For most of us – except candidates studying for technical instructor ratings – this makes no difference at all. In fact, I don't think divemasters are even told it. But it might be worth taking all that inaccuracy stuff into account if one intends to mix gases like nitrox and trimix.

For a specific pressure and temperature, there would be a greater quantity of, let's say oxygen (a highly compressible gas), in a tank than helium (a far less compressible gas).

This might help to explain why, when our calculations for partial-pressure nitrox or trimix filling suggest one outcome, we can easily arrive at something entirely different.

Armed with this little nugget, what does a wise diver do? Let's think about that for a moment: and while we do, let's ask ourselves what else we can learn from Boyle?

It's the behavior described by Boyle's Law that tells us that as a diver descends, the volume of gas he consumes with each breath increases as the pressure outside his body increases. That's to say, the density of the gas being breathed increases. We have open-water divers calculate their way through simple examples to illustrate this point. At 10 metres/33 feet the ambient pressure is about twice what it is on the surface (assuming the dive takes place at sea level) and therefore gas in a scuba diver's lungs will be twice as dense. At 20 metres/66 feet, it'll be three times. At 30 metres/100 feet, it'll be four times and so on.

We can extrapolate from this and state that at 40 metres / 132 feet (five bar or atmospheres) a cylinder containing X litres or Y cubic feet will only last one fifth of the time it would last on the surface. But is there anything else?

THERE IS ALWAYS MORE TO UNDERSTAND

There is more to take into account if we want to understand the effects a denser gas will have on a diver at depth. Ignoring increased gas partial pressures, which lord knows is reason enough to pause and think (and something we will discuss later), let's consider the consequences of the increased work a diver must apply a depth to move a denser gas though a scuba regulator and back out again.

If gas were ideal, and the world was perfect, the work of breathing (WOB) from a scuba regulator during a dive would be no more than breathing here on dry land. But as we've discussed already, gas is not ideal and the world is far from perfect.

As experienced divers we know that breathing from a regulator at depth is not the same as breathing without one on the surface. We can say that the WOB from ANY regulator increases as we take it deeper into the water column.

There was a time when very few scuba regulators were capable of "high-performance." For want of any universal standard to tell us exactly what high-performance meant back then, we – the dive industry – used the criteria set by the US Navy more or less as the default.

A couple of things have changed in the past decade or so... probably a few things. The ones worth noting, which apply to scuba regulators in particular, are that materials and manufacturing methods have improved, standards to gauge performance have been formalized, and machines to perform standard testing on regulators are more readily available.

The CE standard (literally *Conformité Européenne* or *Communauté Européenne*) was originally adopted for products sold within the European Union, but is now recognized worldwide. The CE standard for scuba regulators (EN250:2000) specifies that under test conditions a scuba regulator must be able to move a volume of 62.5 litres (2.2 cubic feet) per minute at an ambient pressure of 6 bars (50 metres/165 feet) while keeping the work of breathing to less than three joules per litre

To understand this standard a little better, we need to know that "volume per inhalation" on the test contraption (almost universally an ANSTI testing apparatus made by a UK-based company), can be varied. To conform to this standard, the volume is set to 2.5 litres, which is a pretty healthy lungful. The number of breaths per minute is set to 25, which is pretty rapid breathing.

This results in 2.5 x 25 = 62.5 l/min. (By the way, if you are more comfortable with imperial units, 62.5 litres is about 2.2 cubic feet.) The density of the gas passing through the machine also varies with depth.

At 50 metres for instance, the machine would be moving 62.5 x 6 litres per minute. That's 375 litres of gas at surface pressure, which is about 13.25 cubic feet per minute, and in either metric or imperial, that is a remarkable volume of gas.

So, what does that mean in terms of diver effort? Well, a Respiratory Minute Volume (RMV) of 62.5 litres per minute would be hard for even a very fit diver to maintain (an average of 35-40 or at most 50 litres a minute seems more likely). So we might conclude that the volume of gas used in the standard test is considerably higher than any realistic average.

Now let's consider the amount of work: less than three joules per litre. For those of you who may have skipped high-school science, a Joule is the amount of work needed to move a force of one newton through one metre.

I remember a physics prof. picking up an apple from his desk and raising it above his head: "That took about one joule of work," he told us. Regardless of whether his on-the-spot example was entirely accurate or not, the image has stayed with me for more than fifty years, so I guess it was a pretty memorable illustration.

So the CE standard means that for every litre of gas no more than three apples will be moved through a metre! I'm not sure if that means anything to you, but essentially, three joules per litre is a moderate WOB.

However, in the general scheme of things scuba, I believe the CE standard is not quite good enough for deep, technical diving.

Meeting the basic standard may be fine for regulators used for open-circuit dives to moderate recreational depths, but if a workload of three joules is the "outside limit" for a high-performance regulator, one might would want it to function more efficiently under normal conditions. For instance, a performance of less than two joules per litre makes many technical divers feel more comfortable. With this level of performance, under an increased demand (when working hard for example), they can be more confident that a regulator could deliver enough gas for their needs, while not contributing too heavily to the buildup of carbon dioxide. In short, it would be more difficult for a deeper diver to over-breathe a regulator that met and then exceeded the CE standard.

And, to complete a long and circuitous stroll through one lesson to be learned from Boyle's Law, it is the potential for hypercapnia (excessive carbon dioxide) that should be a concern. Hypercapnia at depth can quickly progress from rapid breathing to disorientation, panic, hyperventilation, convulsions, and unconsciousness. Alarmingly, there is research that shows even with relatively mild hypercapnia there is a rapid decrease in tolerance to CNS oxygen toxicity in lab rats. Obviously, each of these presents the potential for serious complications on a dive, and if ignored, can eventually cause reactions that could result in a diver's death.

To be fair, both the examples given above of Boyle's Law in action – gas compressibility when mixing breathing gas, and gas density when breathing gas at depth – are not entirely explained by Boyle's Law alone.

To have a handle on real-world gas behavior, and what the total implications of gas behavior might be for a diver, several other factors and peculiarities need to be considered. These are described in a collection of other gas laws and other physical effects including those attributed to: *Messrs.* Charles, Gay-Lussac, Avogadro, Dalton, Henry, Graham, Boltzmann, Van der Waals, Joule–Thomson, et al. The complete list of names is pretty extensive, and for the most part – unless you intend to teach university chemistry majors an intensively detailed course on advanced gas blending techniques – largely unimportant.

What is important is to understand that "stuff" we've been told in our basic classes is simple, is rarely simple. There is always more to learn and always more to understand. And often, when our understanding grows, so too does our perception of what we need to worry about. The fortunate side-effect of this is that our perception of what is totally immaterial grows too, and with it the list of items that can be ignored without prejudice.

With more detailed knowledge, we have an opportunity to turn facts and learned responses into wisdom. We have an opportunity to use insight to make good decisions: decisions that will have a positive effect on our diving. So what specifically can we learn and gain insight on from the greater knowledge we may have gained about Boyle's Law?

Several things but two that really poke their heads above the parapet.

The first is to understand that gas behaves oddly, and will do unexpected things when someone or something crams a whole bunch of it into a small metal cylinder. Therefore, if we are charged with mixing diving gas, we should forego the long-established pencil, paper and calculator route and opt instead to use a reputable mixing program on a tablet or smart phone. Choose one that takes into account gas compressibility and temperature. Most important of all, borrow something from the savvy carpenter's toolbox and measure twice, cut once. Sense-check what your calculations tell you to do. Then, once things are mixed, ANALYSE the results and mark the outside of the cylinder clearly. (A corollary to this is learn to calibrate an analyser properly and understand that fuel cells (oxygen sensors) are notoriously inaccurate and react in odd ways to fluctuations in temperature and moisture.)

Secondly, much is made of narcosis when diving deep. Narcosis can be alleviated in several ways. One is to lessen carbon dioxide build up. To help manage narcosis we can make sure that gas can move easily in and out of regulators that are going to be used at depth.

This means they should be serviced and suitable for deep diving. We might also make the gas to be breathed less dense by adding helium to it. And finally, we might also work on our own ability to actually move a denser gas around at depth. I find it interesting that the several "old-school" deep air divers I have met and spoken with to a person have engaged in some type of respiratory muscle training. Tai-Chi anyone?

We could probably add several side notes at this stage – for example, awareness of swimming induced pulmonary edema (SIPE), and trace toxic gases in breathing mixes – but we'll deal with those other issues in later chapters, so let's wrap up.

An informed and knowledgeable diver is a good thing. Read, listen, learn, and above all other things, keep an open mind. Knowledge is an ever-growing process while wisdom is, rather like common-sense, less common that it should be. We would be well served to make a promise to ourselves and our dive buddies to cultivate more of both.

Chapter Three

TRAINING: More than a plastic card

When, during an October weekend in late 1992, a group of folks started the discussions that culminated in drawing up the eight categories of risk management that serve as the inspiration for this book, none of us can say exactly what they had in mind.

Training had been on the original Sheck Exley five-point list and there it served to remind us that cave diving requires a special program specifically designed to teach participants about the many pratfalls that wait for the unwary in a hard overhead environment. After all, the list of fatal incidents in caves showed that even scuba diving "professionals" such as open water instructors teaching a long list of specialties, were as likely to buy the farm in a cave as the newly minted open-water diver they certified the week before. Without correct and targeted training specifically for cave-diving, death in Exley's time, as it was in the 90s and remains today, an indiscriminate host making no allowances at all for experience in open water. Proficiency there is irrelevant once in a cave.

By the early 1990s, technical diving had already encompassed a lot more than cave diving, and many, many people who had never been inside a hole in the ground, and who had no intention of ever doing "wet rocks diving," called themselves technical divers. These folks needed protection and some guidelines to follow too.

It would be safe to guess that in 1992, the original scope of Exley's caution to get the right training had to be stretched to cover much more than simply getting certified as a cave diver. Certainly today, more than twenty years on, its cautionary advice is intended to cover more than any piece of plastic from XYZ scuba agency.

There is an aphorism that states: never dive beyond the limits of your certification. That's great advice, and certainly a good place to start, but "the Limits of One's Training" should actually be the outcome from a mix of formal coaching and applied experience: and the diving community as a whole does a rather poor job of letting divers know this. Many members of the diving community, beginners through extremely advanced seem to believe that training stops when they get that card handed to them, and have a cloudy understanding of exactly what the limits of their training are, and how best to apply them.

Most certification cards do have a short description of course limits printed on them. These read something like: "Certified to utilize Nitrox and Helium mixes with no greater than 20% He, and up to 100% Oxygen for decompression diving to a maximum depth of 45m/150ft only." (Which is precisely what's printed on a TDI Helitrox Diver card.) Sometimes an additional warning about diving "in conditions better than or equal to those encountered during training" is added, but this still leaves a lot to the imagination. I am sure most experienced divers could dream up all sorts of situations that fit the limits outlined on the card, but which would require vastly different experience and techniques to survive with health and sanity intact.

More to the point, and certainly part of the mission to build a strong buttress against risk, the card – and whatever wall certificate may have come with it – does not make the point that its holder is in effect just beginning his or her 'training' at the specified level. Completing a class earns one an invitation to begin the process of making the skills it taught stick in real life.

THE INSTRUCTOR'S ROLE: The value of tough

One time, an instructor-candidate – someone who had come to me to get trained and certified to teach decompression diving – asked me to tell her the difference between the way a technical diving instructor, which was her immediate goal, and a sport diving instructor, which she already was, each approach teaching the academic portion of a diver ed. program.

She knew I trained both types of instructor, and she may have figured I had some particular insight.

There are lots of things that one could point to, not the least of which is that it's my firm belief that teaching an open-water class to half-a-dozen or so punters off the street – even assuming them all to be highly-internally motivated, intelligent individuals – is more difficult and challenging in so many ways than teaching someone with a couple hundred dives in their log book, a cave-diving or advanced trimix program.

What I explained to her went something like this.

I would be very surprised if an open-water instructor kicked off her first classroom presentation by saying: "If you get this stuff wrong, you can die."

If an instructor candidate did that during an instructor evaluation course, most instructor-trainers would most likely take the candidate aside and explain that a more restrained approach would help to nurture a generally more acceptable learning environment for folks just learning to dive. "Let's try that again, shall we…" is what I might suggest.

However, if a candidate to become a technical instructor kicked off her first classroom session and did not say: "If you get this stuff wrong, you will die." I would expect a similar percentage of instructor-trainers to be just as disappointed.

My explanation was little more long-winded than that but the essential points are there. I believe she understood what I meant and has become a very successful instructor in her own right.

As simplistic as that explanation may seem, it helps to underline how fundamentally different is the approach to presenting limits and risk management at different ends of the teaching/learning spectrum. It's no error in planning or judgement that most technical diving programs start off with a module on accident analysis. Most sport diver programs avoid the topic. However, the role of an instructor in a technical program requires more than being blunt and upfront about the potential dangers that lie ahead; and trying hard to frighten people away.

In this regard alone, effective training and diver education of any advanced diving program requires skillful juggling on the part of the folks who set training standards – the agencies – as well as by the folks on the front lines delivering those programs to end-users – instructors.

For the instructor, juggling the risk/benefit equation presented to students entails a three-handed approach.

On one hand, an instructor has to make sure that whatever the potentially dire consequences associated with the flavor of diving being taught are not trivialized. Part of the value of training is to present the dangers and how best to deal with them.

On the other hand, it's up to the instructor to make sure that actual risks are keep to a minimum and are extremely well managed. Perception is key: students need to be a little on edge. They are doing something unfamiliar and they expect the instructor to throw sinkers and curve balls. In reality the actual circumstances and environment in which the class is held offers plenty of scope for contingencies. The instructor is abundantly comfortable, totally in her comfort zone and ready if something really does go awry during the course.

On yet another hand there has to be some aspect of the course, and the way it is presented, that pushes a student physically and emotionally. Any program aimed at opening participants up to higher risk and higher stress activities, should not be dumbed down. It's rare that everyone in a tough technical program gets a pat on the back and a pass. Certification has to be earned. In doing so, students will find the precise location of their comfort zone's outer edge. An instructor's job is to take them there but to control the experience and to achieve all this without breaking the student's confidence completely.

At this point, it's worth stating that even the most challenging dive program (CCR, cave, scooter, trimix, exploration) remains part of the curriculum for a recreational diver's continuing education. I believe that folks who sign up for scuba training of any type should not be treated like recruits for Special Boat Services. It's the instructor's job to educate and change outlook and behavior without bullying or belittling the accomplishments of their students even when their efforts do not rank as a passing grade.

All instruction in advanced programs must establish an understanding and acceptance in its participants that while diving can be a whole lot of fun, it can be extremely dangerous and totally without mercy to the foolhardy. Establishing this balance – and an understanding that some attrition, some degree of student "failure" is acceptable – is not the only special skill an instructor needs, but it is an important one.

One problem is that the value of formal training has been undermined. Many dive shops and instructors are guilty of devaluing "the brand" in the consumer's eyes by their willingness to cut prices and cut throats. Can we blame Joe Diver for spending money on new gear online rather than the instruction on how to use it when local dive operators bicker among themselves about whose training is the best? Some so-called dive professionals spend as much time bad-mouthing each other – and the programs of other agencies – as doing personal diving and developing personal skills.

As a community, we do a poor job of supporting the community; and it should come as no surprise to us that some divers see no value in continuing diver education. Instead they see it as a money grab, worthless, and easily replaced by a quick google search and ten minutes of reading on a website.

If we expect that to change, we need to change ourselves and show respect for good training regardless of the segment of the alphabet associated with it. The statement: "My training is superior to yours because I am an XYZ diver," is essentially a form of badge-collecting. It's fine to be a fan, but your team cannot always win the cup. When I started diving, BSAC divers where better than PADI divers… or so I heard. Divers trained by both agencies die diving. The issue is not the agencies, at least not theirs alone. The issue is that by putting each other down relentlessly, the message sent out to the average punter does nobody any favors.

So, if you are someone wondering what your next step should be, the best advice I can offer is that when you are sitting down with a cup of tea interviewing a prospective instructor, run away start putting down the guy or gal at the shop around the corner. Look for an instructor who focuses on what you can expect from their program.

PRACTICE BUILDS COMPETENCE: one approach to improving your skillset

In a later chapter, we will discover that the self-assessment process includes asking yourself if you've recently practiced and mastered the appropriate skills for the dive you have planned. Dive skills, both mental and physical, are perishable. Without constant challenge and practice, they tend to dry up and vanish. This is true of every skill but it is especially true when dives involve depth and/or an overhead environment, and the required equipment is more elaborate.

One constant is that good divers understand that training does not stop when an instructor hands them a piece of plastic with a handshake and a congratulatory smile. We call that formalised training, but real training is a balance between doing a class and then going and getting some actual practical experience. Diving with an instructor, at any level, is not the same as diving with your mates… Both events should be fun, both can be learning experience, and both are different aspects of a sort of training continuum.

Statistics available to the dive community tell us that several of the most common triggers seen in events that result in diver deaths cannot be attributed to lack of formal training: perhaps more like a lack of informal training. For example, DAN (Diver's Alert Network) examination of 947 diver deaths showed that more than 380 of them (41 percent) began because of an OOA (out of air) situation.

While we may find this a sorry piece of news, we cannot really blame training or lack of it since every certified diver has been trained – to a greater or lesser extent – on how to avoid and then how to deal with an OOA situation. The community may debate how appropriate and how thorough present levels of training are to prepare open-water divers to deal with an OOA situation or avoid it altogether, but improving a diver's basic training does nothing if the application of those skills is not regularly drilled and practiced.

"Have you practiced the skills you were trained to perform?"

Although I expect most readers will either already be technical divers or be sport divers with near-term aspirations of becoming technical divers, this question is a valid one for any diver to ask themselves: regardless of whether their intended dive is to the officers' mess on the wreck of *HMS Prince of Wales* or the top of the school bus sitting in a few metres of water at their local quarry.

While it's impractical to list skills explicit enough to cover the must-haves for all forms of diving – line management for cave diving, DSMB deployment and management for open-water drift diving for example – we can discuss how to approach the risk management process by building better skills and competence.

Let's start with some priorities. Above all else, safety is the "Prime Directive," and safety is what results from applying all six scuba skills correctly, and following a few uncomplicated rules.

The first rule of diving is to keep breathing. We can expand this a little to read: always have something appropriate to breathe. As naïve as that may sound to some ears, when we want to work out which pieces of a complex diving jig-saw puzzle go where, the first pieces to fit together are the ones that guarantee everyone has plenty of gas to breathe, and that all of that gas in a place where it can be accessed as easily as possible. As long as there is gas to breathe, all other issues are fixable. Nothing to breathe and regardless of how cozy everything else may be, someone is about to experience a serious medical issue.

Close behind on the skills list, and directly related to breathing, is Emotional Control. In simple terms, emotional control is being able to keep it together when the Rottweilers hit the fan. If everyone has something to breathe, all other issues are fixable... that is unless someone panics. Ergo, don't panic. Breathe in slowly, breathe out slowly, repeat until you have a plan to extract you and yours safely away from the current unwelcome situation. If you can control your breathing, you will win.

Panic is not the only emotional enemy. Folks who do a lot of stressing and shouting, are given to emotional roller-coaster rides, who fly into a rage easily, who have problems staying focused when things get hairy, might not be cut out for any high-risk, high-stress endeavor, including scuba diving.

Composure, a calm outlook, Zen, being at one with the world, whatever you want to call it, is the better way to approach advanced diving.

The third skill, equally as important as and related to emotional control, is Situational Awareness. Situational awareness is the skill of knowing how things are supposed to look and feel, and then acting appropriately when things do not look or feel the way they are supposed to. Situational awareness is one part knowledge, one part observation, one part anticipation, and one part having the presence of mind to know what to respond to and what to ignore.

SOME EXAMPLES OF DISASTER SCENARIOS: Please do this at home

I once had a friend describe the end of "the most satisfying dive where nothing went wrong." Three divers surface all laughing loudly and patting each other on the back. One has no dive gear on at all, one has a dry suit and mask and only one fin, and the third has everything the other two lack, plus his own gear, strapped to his person.

What he's describing of course is an example of a group of divers returning from a skills dive taken to an extreme (and perhaps exaggerated a wee bit). It's unnecessary to peel off all your gear including your mask and fins and then buddy-breathe with your partner all the way to the surface from 30 metres down – at least to begin with – but dives where one simulates equipment failures – and other misadventures – can be fun, team-building, and help to maintain basic skills. Here are a few disaster scenarios that you may find useful. As you and your buddy(ies) grow more comfortable, you can multi-task and throw two, three or four "failures" into your training dives.

Let's imagine a group of three divers: Amy, Brian, Claude. They could be rebreather divers, sidemount open-circuit divers, back mount, open-circuit divers, or single-tank back-mounted divers. The fundamentals of skill development are similar since all divers ply their trade in the same medium.

Let's assume Amy, Brian and Claude understand how to manage gas volumes and gas mixes (both issues have their own chapter so we'll skip details here), and they decide to play some "Disaster Scenario" games on dives at their local quarry: a reasonably controlled and stable environment with maximum depth limited to a few metres.

They have long ago read the stats from DAN (Diver's Alert Network) pointing out that the Controlled Emergency Swimming Ascent (CESA) they were taught in their open-water class delivers mixed results. People have killed themselves trying it.

To start with, because of their strong gas management plans, they can't get their heads around a certified diver being so out of touch that they could run out of air AND lose contact with their buddy at the same time thereby making a CESA necessary. In any event, the information from DAN and common-sense informs them that bolting to the surface is the least favored option regardless of circumstances. So for this group, CESA is not in their tool kit. However, they do know that there are alternatives to running out of air that could still result in an unusable primary second stage (such as regulator freeflow, ripped diaphragm, torn mouthpiece, etc.), and these events – and appropriate responses – are what they simulate in their personal training.

All scuba regulators have the potential to freeflow. At some point, if you take a regulator into water, it will misbehave, and freeflowing is what regulators prefer to do when they want to be bad. It is no big deal and our happy trio's disaster scenarios feature this situation often.

Here's one example of how it goes. Brian swims over to Amy, gives her the "ready" signal and pushes the purge button on the second stage that's in her mouth. This causes a cloud of bubbles, which is a pretty good facsimile for a real freeflow. Amy signals Claude she has a problem, which he would be either unsighted or very, very inattentive to have missed because a freeflow is noisy and often spectacular.

As Amy works at signally Claude, she proceeds to reach behind her head to shut down her tank. While she is doing that, Claude swims to her side and offers her his backup regulator, she throws her leaking primary behind her (those bubbles were distracting), breathes gently from Claude's offered alternative, and completes the shutdown. The bubbles 'stop' and all three buddies are able to take stock of their situation and think.

Because their habit is to follow a proper dive plan, they have time to stop, think and act... one thing from their early training that they've decided is golden advice.

With Amy's tank off and the leak dealt with, the dive is "over" but the team has several options.

Both Brian and Claude could take turns donating air to Amy. This allows them leeway to try some alternative options. They have ample gas and plenty of time. One option is to retrieve the problem regulator and see if it will work now. Often, shutting a regulator down for a few beats will "fix" the issue that caused it to freeflow in the first place.

TRY THIS TO CURE A FREEFLOW
Technical divers will often practice a shutdown while keeping the offending second stage in their mouth and after a few seconds rest, they re-open the valve a little and try breathing from it again.

Sometimes, this works and the regulator does not continue to freeflow at all. Sometimes it works for a little and then begins to "creep." Creep is something a diver can sense. The cracking pressure on the second stage lightens up and excess gas just begins to trickle out. It's a good sign that things are about to go pear-shaped once again.

In this case, if Amy sensed things were not going to work out with her regulator, she'd continue to breathe from Claude's alternative second stage regulator (or alternate every few minutes and switch to Brian's). Either way, her reactions have bought her time and independence and freedom from the bolt-to-the-surface reaction that carries so much potential for injury and confusion.

Sidemount divers even practice feathering their primary valves. Feathering is shutting the valve between breaths and cracking it just enough to deliver gas when needed. With a little practice this technique can be done while swimming, ascending, conducting a safety stop and surfacing. The "impacted" diver's buddy needs to be close at hand for the whole exercise, but it's a great confidence builder knowing that you dealt with the problem "solo," and that most of the gas in the effected tank is available.

There are several other scenarios, which Amy, Brian and Claude can dream up and practice to simulate various flavors of malfunction, like multiple failures within the team (more than one person with regulator issues); buddy breathing ascents (normal ascent speed with full safety stop); sharing gas for a horizontal swim for several minutes, during ascent and through safety stops. (Tip: When practicing this, have your SPG in hand and swap roles with your buddy if one person's gas volume starts to get low.)

With a pony bottle as a "prop" (and certainly a redundant gas source is a useful optional extra if these folks expect to graduate to solo diving or technical diving at some point), the options increase.

In my opinion, when single-tank divers use a pony-bottle as an "everything has hit the fan" contingency bottle, the dive team as a whole needs to practice deployment and ascent using it.

Mouthpieces are one of the weak points in both open-circuit and closed circuit equipment. I have seen a rebreather flood almost completely because of nothing more serious than a split in its silicon mouthpiece. And I have read about open-circuit divers panicking and bolting for the surface because of a similar situation or because a silicon mouthpiece came off a second stage.

For the record, both a CCR and regular scuba regulator work just fine without a mouthpiece. The sensation of using one without a mouthpiece is certainly odd but far from impossible. It really just takes some practice… and sometimes a steadying hand if there's any current since without a mouthpiece the only thing keeping the second stage in place is the diver's lips. You might want to try breathing from a second stage without a mouthpiece, but start out with one in water shallow enough to stand up in, and when you get deeper, have the doctored regulator attached to a stage or pony bottle rather than your "real" gas... just in case!

OTHER PIECES OF THE PUZZLE

Most incidents that result in serious injury, death or just some poor soul getting the fright of their life, surfacing and then selling all their dive kit, begin with something very simple. Most seem to be equipment–related issues would be trivial when taken alone and in different circumstances.

I know of one seemingly inconsequential kit failure that resulted in one diver drowning and his buddy suffering serious internal injuries. That a mask coming loose could be the cause of so much grief is staggering. But that's the way of many scuba "accidents."

One domino topples and begins a cascade effect that can easily end in tragedy. It is not possible to simulate realistically the combined effects of task loading, narcosis, and surprise, but practice, constant practice will help build resilience to the influence of all three.

Task loading is a function of diving itself, but can be exacerbated by diving with new pieces kit, in new surroundings, with an unfamiliar buddy or with a poor kit configuration.

Narcosis is an odd variable related to nitrogen depth but also attributable to so many other factors, including high-stress, high-workload. And surprise is a function of the real-world getting in the way of the world most of us would like to live in.

Surprise can never be totally eliminated but situational awareness coupled with a good contingency plan, dampens its ability to shock.

Perhaps the most harmful mistake a diver can make when a piece of equipment breaks is to focus on it when the focus should be elsewhere. In other words, to forego situational awareness and to lose sight of primacy.

I have seen people get focused on a something as petty as a jammed reel. This is relatively common in both cave and advanced wreck classes when students are trying their hardest to get things perfect for their instructor. In these situations, a jammed reel is a godsend. Instructors pray for stuff like this. Here's how a jammed reel scenario could go in a typical class. (I am pretty sure many of you who have completed a cave or advanced wreck will identify with this.)

So, the reel jams on the way home when the dive has been called either on time or gas. The "last" diver in the group looks down at the jammed reel, pauses for a few seconds, and as he does so, his buddy swims off without looking back (around a corner, through a doorway, whatever). The diver with the reel fixates for a few more seconds on the "problem" and tries to correct it.

Often, a reel jams because line is loose and wraps itself between the spool and the axle. With a few reels, this can be fixed in the water, but with most, it takes more time than most divers have when exiting a called dive. It is a task to pass time during a decompression stop perhaps, but not when swimming. In any event, trying to fix it with your buddy out of sight during an exit is the wrong thing to do... ALWAYS. This is just my opinion, but I feel pretty strongly about it in a cave and much more so inside a wreck. Caves and wrecks are somewhat similar environments. Some divers lump them together as "hard overheads" but wrecks provide way more opportunity for things to mess up horribly. Caves have their special threats, often related to the sheer distance from fresh air, but wrecks are spectacularly unpredictable. Wrecks are organic entities and a whole order of magnitude more difficult in many ways than caves.

I dive and teach in both and am way more on edge inside a wreck because there is no way to guarantee that the way you came in will be the best way to get out. That's not always the case, but I can honestly say that I have never been lost in a cave, even when laying new line... I have second-guessed my location in a wreck, even with a reel in my hand and a continuous line to the exit. Wrecks

A small primary reel from Light Monkey. An exceptionally functional and clean design that is difficult to "bird's nest" and slick to use.

are way more challenging to navigate, and offer a line many, many places to get trapped and abraded.

Back to our scenario: a bird's nested reel + fixation on the wrong issue + buddy out of sight = potential for a real issue. Add one more thing to this scenario and BINGO: there is a possibility for a really nicely packaged "learning opportunity."

For example, the instructor at this point, swims behind the poor student who is fiddling with his reel and who is fixated on it rather than keeping in touch with his team, and 1) puts a loop of line around some part of the diver's kit to simulate entanglement 2) shuts of the diver's primary light 3) pushes a purge button on one of the diver's regulators to simulate freeflow... or a really challenging instructor will do all three! With an experienced instructor leading the dance and available to help out if needed, any combination of these vignettes would be stressful for the diver. While alone in a real-world situation, the outcome could easily be a calamity waiting to unleash a little personal hades.

The last time you earned a certification card – assuming you did not simply buy it – you may have been told it signified that you now have a licence to learn. To be clear and less banal, the translation for that particular phrase is that the piece of plastic changing hands means nothing unless seat-of-the-pants disaster scenarios such as the ones outlined above have been drilled (regularly and recently). Although they lack the real-world ingredients of surprise, close panic, real stress, simulated events and drills do help divers learn the correct options for a safe end to their dive.

Having equipment go pear-shaped, can be a Road to Damascus moment. There are some responses that are potentially the correct ones in real-life, but which are ill-advised for simulation: kinking the offending low-pressure hose to slow a freeflow from draining a tank when there is no alternative might be one example, since it usually ruins the hose. However, drills, especially with buddies who are good actors and who have the diving skill to make a scenario look, feel and taste authentic, will help to give your 'personal' on-going training veracity.

REACTION CHEAT SHEET
"Total Risk" is a function of probability multiplied by possible outcome. For a newer open-water diver, there is, generally speaking, a higher probability of them bobbing to the surface at the end of the dive as a result of an uncontrolled buoyant ascent than there is for a similar event to happen to a trained technical diver.

However, the possible outcomes of this type of event for each type of diver are very different. This informs the way risk is assessed for each.

The level of total risk for specific events therefore depends almost entirely on the circumstances and there are few events that we can point to and say with certainty, "… is the correct response." Bearing this in mind, the chart opposite is a "cheat sheet" listing calamities and possible solutions. It is based on one I use for students enrolled in overhead programs. It is not published here as a how-to so much as a template for you to develop your own version of it as you continue your training.

It is also not the full skills sheet but a partial one. Your mileage will vary and if you intend to use something like this to supplement your diving and dive planning, I suggest you start from the ground up or surface down as it were. Figure out what can possibly go wrong, and what will put it right.

If you are embarking on a technical diving program, your actual course dives will help to inform what you should write on your personal Cheat Sheet. If you cannot think of a good response to a situation, go find an instructor and work with him or her to fix that deficit; or stay away from situations in which the probability of the event happening is high.

INTRO TO CAVE, OPEN-CIRCUIT, SIDEMOUNT TWO OR THREE PERSON TEAM	
SCENARIO	*POTENTIAL SOLUTION*
LOST MASK	DEPLOY BACKUP, CHECK GAS, CONTINUE DIVE OR END DIVE
LIGHT FAILURE	DEPLOY BACKUP, CHECK GAS, SIGNAL END DIVE OR TURN DIVE
LOSS OF VISIBILITY	FIND LINE, OK LINE, CONTACT BUDDY, HEAD OUT (CHECK DIRECTION) CHECK GAS, WHEN VIS RETURNS
LOST LINE	STOP, THINK, THEN EXECUTE LOST LINE DRILL, FIND LINE, ATTACH COOKIE, CHECK GAS (+ PPO2), HEAD OUT
LOST BUDDY	SECURE LINE, CHECK GAS (+ PPO2), LOOK FOR SIGNS (LIGHT, SILT, LOOK UP AND ALL AROUND), WAIT APPROPRIATE TIME, ATTACH COOKIE, EXIT
REGULATOR FREEFLOW	SIGNAL TEAM AND MODERATE GAS LOSS, ATTEMPT FIX, NO FIX POSSIBLE THEN DEPLOY ALTERNATIVE, NO ALTERNATIVE, FEATHER VALVE, SIGNAL END OF DIVE, EXIT SPG IN SIGHT
DECO REGULATOR FREEFLOW	FEATHER VALVE, SIGNAL BUDDY, BUDDY BREATHE IF NECESSARY. CONTINGENCY DECO SCHEDULE AS LAST RESORT
LP FREEFLOW (WING/SUIT)	DISCONNECT LP HOSE, NO FIX, TURN OFF FIRST STAGE, CHECK GAS VOLUME, SIGNAL TURN DIVE OR END DIVE
TANGLED REEL/LINE	WRAP LINE AROUND SPOOL, EXIT NORMALLY. or TIE-OFF REEL LEAVE EXIT NORMALLY. FIX TANGLE AT SAFETY STOP OR IN DAYLIGHT
ENTANGLEMENT	STOP, SIGNAL BUDDY, ACCESS SITUATION, CHECK GAS VOLUME, THINK, ACT, REPAIR CUT LINE, USE DIRECTIONAL ARROWS TO POINT OUT
WING MALFUNCTION	INFLATE ORALLY. IF WING RUPTURED ORIENT TO MAINTAIN SOME LIFT, USE ALTERNATE BUOYANCY, USE BUDDY FOR LIFT
DRYSUIT FLOOD	SIGNAL BUDDY, EXIT IN CONTACT WITH BUDDY, EXIT WATER WITH CARE
LOW ON GAS	SIGNAL BUDDY, SHOW SPG, BREATHE FROM BUDDY A FOR 50 BAR, BUDDY B FOR 50 BAR, EXIT. KEEP SUFFICIENT VOLUME TO INFLATE WING ON SURFACE

And above all, please remember that common-sense and thoughtful analysis during all stages of your diving will go a long, long way to keeping you out of harm's way.

Ask questions, always. When you are told: "we do this this way," ask why and if the reason does not seem to make sense, continue to probe until either a light

goes on above your head or the "expert" trying to convince you admits they have no idea.

Training at the level where you and your buddies are going to crank up the potential for injury is required and is an on-going process. Diving in an overhead environment, virtual or real, is easy without training until something goes wrong and then your chances of dying increase exponentially. A structured training program will give you the tools to build the skills to deal with something going wrong.

Most of all, once that program is over, if you do intend to continue, take personal responsibility for the application of what you learned, and respect the limits of your skills and where their usefulness ends.

Chapter Four

GAS SUPPLY: always have something to breathe

Of the eight guidelines for successful risk management, the importance of the fourth – guaranteeing an abundant gas supply – should be the easiest for all of us to grasp since it has without doubt the most straight-forward elevator pitch: if you can't breathe you die.

You don't even have to be a scuba diver to understand the sense contained in that laconic piece of advice; or why it's wise to put emphasis on making sure we have enough gas to finish the dive – plus a little extra – even before the dive begins. Anyone who draws breath gets what this guideline has to teach us about safety. But unfortunately, every year – including this one – a number of poor saps die inside a wreck or deep in a cave, or even on a reef in open water because they ran out of "air."

To be blunt and to make sure each of us is going to be happy taking the same fork in the road as we start on this leg of our journey through risk management, let's come to an understanding: there is no excuse for running out of gas. None. Unless there is an asteroid strike or some other equally unlikely event that bars one's passage back to fresh air, there is nothing that should result in a diver running out of gas. Nothing. It is unacceptable. Even a diver alone in the water has no excuse. To allow oneself to run out of air is a damning commentary on one's basic understanding of dive protocols and a demonstration that a very basic survival skill is absent.

Running out of air is not an accident: it is oversight. But people do it, and with alarming frequency! Obviously, something must be wrong, and I have to assume the issue is failure in the way the diving community regards, promotes and underscores the most basic canons and theories dealing with in-water survival. For this situation to persist, we must have a whole segment of divers, old and new, thinking they can breathe water.

I was tempted to write that there is a failure in training, but the problem, and problem it is, is systematic. It may begin with curriculum design and training, but it includes failures in organization, community awareness, process, and the growth of a culture that turns a blind-eye to unsafe practices. Not only do we teach inadequate gas management skills to new divers, that inadequacy is sustained by instructors, agencies, dive operators, diving literature, and fellow divers industry wide.

In the following few pages, I hope to show you how to calculate your gas volume requirements – literally, how much gas does it take to keep someone like you happy and alive for every minute underwater – and to give you a few suggestions for ways to carry that gas with you on your dives. While these calculations and kit configurations are commonly used by technical divers, they can, and I believe should, be adopted by all divers. I am a particular fan of the "rule" that suggests any and all dives to 30 metres or beyond (100 feet or deeper) require the diver to have a redundant gas source [other than his/her buddy]. I will try to make a convincing argument to readers while explaining why and how.

THE GROUND RULES: SAC

For the time-being, let's forget rules of thirds and rock-bottom requirements. Let's focus on the absolute basics and let's get clear on a couple of definitions.

First, we will need to do some simple calculations about gas volumes, and to start, we need to agree on a baseline: some kind of an average consumption rate that will work as a starting point, and from which anyone who wants to create individual guidelines based on a more personal figure can depart.

On open-circuit, at rest and on the surface, the average male will "consume" around 14 litres or half a cubic foot of gas every minute. For the rest of this exercise, we'll refer to this as 'average SAC rate.' SAC in this case means Surface Air Consumption.

Different divers each have different lung capacities (often referred to as vital volume), and breathing patterns differ greatly too, but average SAC is a decent starting point and it's been used to illustrate gas supply needs to students in advanced and technical programs for decades. At some point, you will want to plug-in your personal SAC rate, but bear with me for a few paragraphs and let's use 14 litres and 0.5 cubic feet as our default throughout the rest of this chapter.

In addition, we will work through the following examples in both metric and imperial units. Later on, when we discuss options for rebreather diving, specifically closed-circuit rebreather diving, I'll be using metric and only metric values.

The reasoning for this omission is simply that all calculations for diving are easier with metric units; however, I speak both metric and American Customary Units (usually called imperial units). That being said, I have never used or been asked to use imperial units when diving rebreathers… frankly, I do not know how to!

Also, if mathematics and anything to do with arithmetic makes your head spin, relax. There will be tables and a "fudge factor" technique that requires you to do no calculations whatsoever. For those of you that prefer to work "old school," you can do the calculations longhand, and plug in numbers from real dives rather than fudging.

The good news is that it is totally unnecessary for anyone to remember things like the Trapezoidal Rule or the differences between and typical applications for derivatives and definite integrals.

Gas volume calculations are simple arithmetic, so if you can work out how much tip to leave after dinner in a restaurant with friends, you can calculate your personal gas consumption needs. And if using a calculator confuses you, there's an app for your phone to help with gas planning: really, there is.

SAC should be viewed as a constant. The actual rate at which we belt through a tank of nitrox at depth is influenced by many, many variables, and we are going to take those into account. But to answer the "How much gas do I need" question with any degree of accuracy, we must begin with a constant.

We will use the average 14 l/min (litres per minute) or 0.5 cfm (cubic feet per minute) for the time-being. These actually describe very similar needs since there are about 28.3 litres in a standard cubic foot, so take your pick, litres or cubic feet. At this point, your preference will not influence the validity of what follows.

Boyle's Gas Law informs us that as a diver goes deeper, the ambient pressure around her increases. When she is diving on scuba, her lungs stay the same size as they were on the surface, but to fill them she has to overcome the increased pressure of the water between her and the surface, and this means that the gas she draws into her lungs via her regulator must be more dense than it would be on the surface.

At 10 metres or 33 feet the ambient pressure is about twice that at sea level. Therefore, the gas in her lungs will have to be twice as dense; at 20 metres or 66 feet that gas has to be three times the density; at 30 metres or 99 feet, four times; 40 metres or 132 feet; five times and so on.

Consumption rate increases with depth... average SAC every 5 m / 16-17 ft				
DEPTH METRES	DEPTH FEET	AMBIENT (bar /ata)	METRIC (l/min)	IMPERIAL (cfm)
SURFACE	SURFACE	1.0	14	0.50
5	16	1.5	21	0.75
10	33	2.0	28	1.00
15	50	2.5	35	1.25
20	66	3.0	42	1.50
25	82	3.5	49	1.75
30	99	4.0	56	2.00
35	115	4.5	63	2.25
40	132	5.0	70	2.50
45	147	5.5	77	2.75
50	165	6.0	84	3.00
55	180	6.5	91	3.25
60	198	7.0	98	3.50
Fudge factor: When actual depth is between two values, use next deepest depth to calculate gas requirements (i.e. Use 35 m for 31 m dive).				

This lineal increase directly affects every open-circuit diver's consumption rate. Technically, their SAC remains constant, but the increased depth modifies their needs and their per minute requirement doubles, triples, quadruples and so on as they pass each waypoint on their way to their target depth (see table above).

SAC IS ONLY PART OF THE STORY

The table shows us that the volume of gas needed each minute increases as we get deeper in the water column; but it only tells us part of the story. SAC is a measurement of our required consumption on the surface.

On the surface, most of us are a little more relaxed, less stressed and doing a little less work than when we are wearing dive kit and swimming around in the water. Consequently, in addition to the modification we have to make to the average SAC to compensate for depth and density, we have to add a **dive factor** (DF) to bring the estimated consumption rate up to a realistic level.

The DF is intended to take into account the combined effects of thermal stress, workload (swimming against a current, etc.), diminished visibility, nerves, and all the other factors and stressors that we encounter on the average dive. It lumps them altogether in one place as it were and is more convenient than trying to account for each as an individual factor.

The DF scale in the table shown below runs from 1.2 times normal consumption to an upper limit of four times normal consumption. These numbers are highly speculative and how these apply from dive-to-dive and day-to-day will vary considerably. I have attempted to catalog the conditions and factors relating to each DF but these are arbitrary. DF ratings for you and your buddies may vary. Use these as a starting point and with common-sense, practice and some real data to check against, you will develop a knack for applying the correct DF to your dives.

Your application will be different to mine, but I find a DF of 1.4 works well for an average dive in warm water and a dive site I am familiar with. Add a camera to those variables and the DF is now 1.6 or 1.7. Take away the camera but throw in current and unfamiliarity with the site, and my DF might easily be 2.0. In fairness, if I thought a dive warranted a DF above 2.5, I'd think about diving someplace else. DFs of 3 or 4 are for exceptional circumstances such as bailout from a CCR after a scrubber malfunction and CO_2 break-through, or gas sharing with a buddy after massive equipment failure.

The combination of SAC modified for depth multiplied by a suitable DF will give a good estimation of the per minute gas consumption rate for an actual dive. For example, a typical dive in one region where I do a lot of teaching is an almost square profile dive to a moderate-sized wreck in mild current with a sand bottom at 28 metres (that's about 90 feet). The visibility is fair to good, and the water is warm even though I dive in a light-weight drysuit.

DIVE FACTOR (DF) WORKING CHART			
DF	**ENVIRONMENT**	**L/MIN**	**CF/MIN**
1.0	Pool-like conditions	14	0.5
1.2	Warm water, calm, familiar, very light kit	15.4	0.6
1.4	Warm dive, familiar site and buddy, "Normal dive"	19.6	0.7
1.6	Test dive (new kit, new buddy), familiar site and conditions, or moderate work load	22.4	0.8
1.8	Current, cool water, moderate workload, unfamiliar site	25.2	0.9
2.0	High-workload	28	1.0
2.2	Exceptional conditions such as flooded DS in cool water	30.8	1.1
2.5	Extremely high workload, high stress, strong current, dramatic events	35	1.25
3.0	Uncomfortable conditions, almost impossible workload, CO2 break-through	42	1.5
4.0	Volume required by two trained divers sharing gas under controlled circumstances (some regulators would be challenged to deliver this much gas)	56	2.0

Armed with the information in the tables above, we can work through the basic "calculations" for air consumption using the fudge factor built into the table showing modified SAC for depth. The maximum depth is 28 metres, which requires us to use the values for the next deepest. So we use 30 metres and have a small degree of extra conservatism in our calculations. This tactic is especially recommended when you start estimating gas consumption without any hard data (actual numbers from past dives) to sense-check against.

Our consumption rate table gives us a base consumption rate at 30 metres or 99 feet of 56 l/min or 2.0 cfm. Great. Now for the Dive Factor, and my suggestion, given the parameters mentioned, would be a DF of 1.6, and that is what we need to multiply our modified SAC by.

Let's see: 1.6 x 56 = 89.6 l/min. In imperials units that's, 1.6 x 2.0 = 3.2 cfm. Now let's remember that this is an ESTIMATED consumption rate. On the actual dive – at various waypoints – we should keep track of our actual use compared to our estimated use. We'll get to waypoints in detail in the chapters on Exposure and Operations, but a waypoint is a specific "landmark" during the dive or a specified elapsed time, as in "when we have been down for eight minutes, we should have used X litres or cubic feet of gas."

Once we have an estimate of how much gas a diver will need for each minute spent on the wreck, we can now make a realistic estimate of how long they can stay down with the gas they have in their tank!

This particular dive site is visited by scores of sport divers, and the vast majority of them use very similar kit. We'll work within the boundaries common to that particular configuration.

A so-called aluminum 80 (an aluminum cylinder with a rated nominal volume of 80 cubic feet at a working pressure usually 3000 psi). Eighty cubic feet at a consumption rate of 3.2 cfm is going to last about 25 minutes before it becomes completely empty.

For a metric user, an aluminum 80 is a fraction bigger than 11 litres and a fill means it's pumped up to 207 bar. Therefore, we have 11.1 litres (the tank's actual wet volume or 'size') times 207 bar to give us 2297 litres in the tank waiting to be used. At a consumption rate of 90 l/min (I rounded up a smidge), that's around 25 minutes. No surprise that both calculations give us 25 minutes to empty since time is common to both metric and imperial users… luckily.

So, the absolute maximum bottom time for an average diver in the conditions and depth of our example is 25 minutes. However, since we are trying to avoid running out of air, a 25-minute dive is out of the question. We have to save a portion of our gas to ascend, complete a safety stop and have some gas reserved for contingency.

HOW MUCH RESERVE IS ENOUGH: the balance between safe and dodgy
Our sport diving example presents us with a problem: no gas reserves. Our diver cannot possibly squeeze a 25-minute dive out of the volume of gas in her tank. She will need to cut her dive short to have enough gas to ascend, conduct the required stop(s), and surface. Also, she must plan some reserve gas to donate to their buddy in case they have some sort of gas emergency during the dive.

Common advice to a sport diver is: "Back on the boat with X bar or X psi in your cylinder." As far as it goes, not necessarily poor advice. But if you want to follow this advice, how long will your dive be and at what tank pressure do you need to begin your ascent to arrive at the safety stop with enough gas to finish it and get to the surface with the stated reserve intact?

There are several ways to plan gas volume around a simple sport dive to 30 metres / 100 feet or less. Some methods are more conservative than others, and some barely conservative at all. We'll look at one that requires very little work with pencil, paper and a calculator: Modified Thirds. There are many other methods and to some extent they all "work." Each carries with it a degree of reassurance and security, and is a vast improvement in terms of risk management over "playing it by ear."

Many divers who have been trained to estimate gas needs before a dive, like and prefer to use modified thirds because of its simplicity. This method requires little calculation, and leaves a reserve of extra gas should something go amiss while at depth or during the ascent. It is aimed at recreational sport divers rather than more advanced technical divers, because it does have limitations. It is not super conservative, and so is not really suitable for more complex dives and certainly not for overhead diving of any type. It also requires that both buddies (or all three buddies when diving a three-person team) are using similar-sized tanks filled to very similar pressures at the start of the dive.

Deeper dives and divers with dissimilar tanks and starting volumes really call for the techniques used in technical diving. There are also other more conservative methods for sport divers, but these require a little more work with numbers and a calculator and therefore are more difficult to apply.

Modified thirds is the easiest method by far and simply means that sport divers begin their ascent when one diver's SPG shows that only one-third of his (or the common) starting pressure remains.

For the wreck dive we used as an example above, we can extrapolate that the maximum bottom-time allowable under the guidance of Modified Thirds would be about two-thirds of the maximum time available to our divers. Since we calculated the maximum time to empty a tank was about 25 minutes, using only two-thirds of that volume of gas would most likely translate to two-thirds of 25 minutes: which is between 16 and 17 minutes.

So we have learned that a diver with an Average SAC, using an aluminum 80 and diving to a little less than 30 metres (less than 100 feet) in water conditions that warrant a Dive Factor of 1.2, should be able to rack up 16 or 17 minutes bottom time, and still have a healthy reserve of gas. Operationally, we could brief divers wanting to do this dive by explaining that the dive will end when the first of them reaches a specific pressure (about 70 bar or 1000 psi) or when the elapsed dive time adds up to 16 to 17 minutes: whichever comes first.

If we were doing a dive which we began by dropping down an anchor line and swimming, let's say west along a reef wall, we would plan to turn and start heading back to the anchor after around eight minutes (given no real currents).

This simplified method tends to work fine, leaves a reserve should a buddy have a gas leak or entanglement or other minor problem, but it is limited in its scope.

Let's look in more detail about how reserve gas works.

Diver A and Diver B started their dive with 207 bar / 3000 psi in their same-sized cylinders. (In this example, we'll assume aluminum 80s and also that the temperature of the gas in each is the same, the gas mix is that same, and therefore the actual amount of gas in each is close to being the same). Just prior to diver A's pressure gauge showing a remaining pressure of 68-70 bar / 1000 psi, he signals his buddy to finish the dive and the two of them begin their ascent. Diver B has more gas than diver A by default (a safe assumption since if that were not the case, diver B would have signalled an end to the dive earlier than her buddy).

The ascent from 30 metres / 100 feet (the maximum suggested depth for this method) to a safety stop at 4.5 - 4 metres or 15 feet, should take at least three minutes. During this first segment of their ascent – given average SAC, a relaxed attitude and good conditions – both divers will consume around 127 litres or about 4.5 cubic feet of gas. (To arrive at this figure long-hand, take the ambient pressure at a mid-point between the bottom and the safety stop, use average SAC, a DF of 1.2 and calculate a total time of three minutes of travel.)

At the safety stop, each diver will breathe approximately 68 litres or 2.6 cubic feet of gas. (Again the long-hand method is to multiply the average SAC modified by a DF of 1.2, by the ambient pressure at the safety stop (1.45 bar or ata), by the duration of the stop (three minutes).) All this gives us a total gas requirement of 200 litres for ascent to the safety stop plus a three-minute stop, plus a few litres to get from the safety stop to the surface. For the PSI diver, the gas used for the whole ascent within the same parameters will be around 7.25 cubic feet.

The approximate volume of the reserve which each had when they left the bottom was 760 litres or 26 cubic feet. Their requirements to make the controlled and recommended ascent outlined above are 200 litres and 7.25 cubic feet respectively, hence, they have ample to get themselves up. The additional "air cushion" makes allowances for something going totally pear-shaped at depth or on the way to the surface requiring diver A and B to share gas. Even with the additional consumption of a stressed diver, there should be ample gas using this method to get both to the surface after a normally-paced ascent and safety stop. The ability to conduct a normal ascent is critical.

Following this method virtually guarantees that even with a gas emergency (a buddy suddenly bleeding gas from a freeflowing regulator for instance), two divers breathing from one cylinder can ascend normally, complete a safety stop and reach the surface without the decompression injuries (DCI) that can be the result of rapid, panicked bolts for the surface from depth.

So, just to recap Modified Thirds: 30 metres, 100 feet or less, same starting pressure, same tank, no overhead, no required decompression.

THINGS TO REMEMBER

For most recreational sport dives, we only need to be mindful of a couple of numbers: the turn-around pressure and the pressure at which we simply have to be ready to start our ascent. It really is that simple.

Something that seems to make sport divers uneasy is that gas planning is "difficult." It certainly is not, and more importantly, once done, it's done. Write down the numbers, commit them to memory. One can reuse the same numbers over and over again for dives to similar or shallower depths.

On extremely shallow dives, the volume of reserve gas to get you and a buddy back to safety will perhaps be less than one third of your starting volume. In these cases, let's say you dive at a local site where everything interesting is no deeper than 20 metres / 70 feet. Use the long-hand method outlined above and in the next section of this chapter to work out how much gas it would take to get you and a buddy to the surface, and keep that aside. That becomes your new reserve.

When in doubt, be conservative. It will be great fun to tell your great grandkids that you always surfaced with 'too much' gas.

Before your dive:

- Confirm your tank pressure, and your buddy's. State to each other the turnaround pressure and the pressure you will have when you leave the bottom.
- Do a proper buddy check and make sure air is all the way on (no closed a half turn nonsense), regulators work (wet breathe) and that back-up regulators are stowed where you can get them in an emergency.

- Perform a proper bubble check on your buddy and have them check you out. You are looking for any leaks but particularly on hose connections and o-rings.

During the dive:

- Monitor your gas pressure frequently. A good diver has a pretty good idea of what his or her SPG is going to display before they look at it. Keep track of your consumption and compare the real-world pressure drop to your dive plan estimate. Adjust your dive accordingly.
- Keep your own and your buddy's turn pressures and ascent pressures in mind. Write them on a slate or in your wet notes for reference, and check them.
- If you should be diving with someone new, gas management is the first and last item you need to discuss. If they don't want to listen or ignore the safe guidelines, thumb the dive and find a buddy who does not have unsafe habits.

USING ADDITIONAL REDUNDANCY: the maligned and misunderstood pony bottle

I would guess that most dive instructors, especially those who teach technical programs, get regular requests from divers to explain how to "use" a pony bottle, how to configure it so it's not in the way, and which size pony bottle is "right" for them.

These are great questions because any diver who intends to dive deeper than 30 metres / 100 feet should carry a redundant source of gas. A dive buddy is supposed to represent the first line of backup, and a well-trained and well-practiced buddy is a great resource in the event of some major gas emergency.

However, the best strategy is that whenever practical strive to have a backup for your backup. In this regard, redundant air via a redundant delivery system offers a huge cushion. Indeed, so compelling is the argument in favor of carrying a pony and using it as an emergency bailout / buddy bottle that a growing number of sport divers use one on all dives whether deep or shallow.

The question of size is perhaps the first question to answer because how to rig and use a pony bottle depends to a large extent on its size.

When estimating how much backup we might need in the event of a massive gas failure in our "primary system" (our normal tank and regulator), we first factor in a full minute at maximum depth to get things sorted and to gather our wits before starting the ascent. This is a critical element in ensuring adequate gas. Gas buys time and having extra time will help calm things down and allows us to Stop, Think, then Act.

With this in mind, let's revisit the table for SAC adjusted for depth. Since we are still talking about recreational sport diving, the limit for maximum depth is around 40 metres or 132 feet. I suggest using this depth since the volume of gas and size of tank required to meet the needs of a bailout from this depth will more than cover dives to lesser depths. Therefore, the pony bottle for these deep sport dives can be the simple default for all sport dives.

The ambient pressure at 40 metres / 132 feet is five bar and therefore the average per minute consumption will be 70 litres or 2.5 cubic feet. Let's also apply a realistic dive factor.

Since a pony bottle is only deployed in times of stress, we need to use a DF for that first minute that reflects high-stress. The norm for this application is a DF of 2.5, which translates into 175 litres or 6.25 cubic feet for that critical first minute!

At this point if you have never done this type of worst-case scenario planning before and are beginning to question the veracity of ads extoling the virtues of those tiny emergency cylinders of "spare" compressed air: good.

After the first minute, we calculate a normal ascent rate (nine metres or 30 feet per minute) up to a safety stop. That journey – about 35 metres/ 117 feet – will take about four minutes. Once again, to help simplify the calculations, we use the ambient pressure at the midpoint between maximum depth and the safety stop, which in this case will be 3.22 bar. We also drop the DF to 2.0. So we have ascent time x SAC x ambient pressure x DF, which equals 360 litres or about 13 cubic feet of gas.

Now for the safety stop. Even when a dive is within the no decompression limits, there is a strong suggestion from most experts that a five-minute stop is indicated after a dive to maximum depth. So the consumption for a five-minute stop at 4.5 metres or 15 feet with a mild DF of 1.2 adds up to a total of 122 litres or 4.35 cubic feet. Finally we have to factor in a little gas for the last part of the ascent to the surface. Therefore, the best estimate is that a controlled ascent following an emergency at depth will require at least 680 litres or close to 25 cubic feet of breathable gas!

It's the considered opinion of most divers who have experienced a real gas emergency at depth in real-world dive conditions – suddenly dark, gloomy, unfriendly and unsettling – that these numbers are neither exaggerated nor inflated.

When something bad happens at great depth, there is no such thing as a plan that is too conservative or too careful. The risks of drowning, embolism, decompression sickness and various other ailments that can result from stark panic and ballistic ascents are very real and totally unforgiving. The alternative to a controlled normal ascent are simply not worth considering.

Clearly then, the "right" pony is one that holds at least 680 litres or 25 cubic feet. Because of its general usefulness in sport diving and technical diving (for carrying decompression gas), its buoyancy characteristics, ease of deployment, and attractive cost compared to smaller tanks, many divers invest in an aluminum 40 (nominal capacity 40 cubic feet / 1200 litres) as the best "emergency" pony bailout/buddy bottle.

Two final words on the topic of pony bottles before we move on to gas volume management for more advanced diving. The gas carried in a pony bottle is contingency gas. It should never be factored into the gas volume requirements for a dive. It is there for emergency use only. It's like the fire extinguisher that sits beside the hob in your kitchen: you hope you will never need it.

If your dive plan calls for more gas than you can carry in a regular primary scuba cylinder – an aluminum 80 for example – then the total kit configuration for the dive needs to be reconsidered and calls for an additional primary cylinder or a high-volume primary cylinder such as a steel 15 litre / 120 cubic-foot tank. Your bailout is not a factor in your non-contingency gas management plans. It does not extend bottom time.

Also, a bailout/buddy bottle is useless if it does not deliver breathable gas faultlessly. The regulator needs to be the best one you own, not some cheap rubbish from the discount bin at your local dive shop or local scuba swap. The valve, regulator and SPG must also be tested before every dive. Do not take for granted that it is filled and in working order. Analyse and label its contents, check the pressure and wet-breathe the regulator just in case it's needed: because when it is needed, it will be needed in earnest.

TECHNICAL DIVING: The rule of thirds in overhead environments

OK, so now we can look into the gas volume management method technical divers employ for dive to any depth, dives in hard and soft overheads, divers with dissimilar cylinders and/or dissimilar starting pressures, and staged decompression dives.

A fundamental difference between sport and technical diving is the way limits are approached in the water and during dive planning. At no point is this more evident to an outsider looking in than with gas volume management. Technical divers simply carry more gas in more tanks!

One reason that technical divers need to be assured that they have sufficient gas to keep breathing for every stage of their dives – including those long ascents to decompress – is theirs is a world where rapid ascents to the surface kill and maim.

METHOD TO FIND YOUR SAC RATE

We could use average SAC rate to plan a technical dive; however, most experienced technical divers know their personal consumption rate and would prefer to use it. If you do not know yours – technical diver or not – you might want to invest some time in discovering what it is.

There are two popular methods to calculate your personal SAC. I've used both: they both deliver very, very similar results. (And a note to those divers who are seriously thinking about semi-closed and fully closed-circuit rebreathers, you will be a step ahead if you start your training knowing your SAC rate.)

The first method involves no diving, but it will generate strange looks from family and friends. As we've discussed, SAC is a resting consumption rate for a person at surface pressure; so, grab a cylinder of breathable gas (and preferably a small cylinder that will register a considerable pressure drop), make a note of the time, make a note of the starting pressure, and stick a reg. in your mouth and a mask on your face (or block your nose somehow).

Now stroll around the garden, watch or listen to your favorite show, music, podcast, whatever. You'll get the best results if you move around a little but do not jump on a stationary bike or elliptical and workout. Sit down for a while, get up sweep the floor, fold laundry, any light activity will be fine.

Breathe from the tank for at least 15 minutes, and if possible longer. Note the pressure drop and finish time. Calculate how much gas you used per minute! You now know your personal SAC, but remember, this is a resting rate. You have to modify it by applying a DF!

To get any meaningful results from this method and the next, you will also need to know how to translate pressure drop in your chosen scuba cylinder into a more meaningful unit such as litres or cubic feet.

For those of us who use the metric system, nothing could be easier since tanks are classified in "wet" volume: for example a 10 litre cylinder has an internal volume of ten litres. That means for each drop in one bar on the SPG, 10 litres of gas have been used.

So, let's say I walk about my garden pulling weeds for 23 minutes breathing from a 10 litre tank. (It's OK, I live in a remote area surrounded by spruce, fir, maple, ash, birch and poplar trees... my neighbors can't see into my garden.)

When I started out, the SPG read 125 bar. After 23 minutes the SPG reads a smidge over 100 bar. I have used about 25 bar of gas from a 10 litre cylinder, and therefore I have consumed about 250 litres of gas (10 x 25 = 250). By dividing that number by the number of minutes – 23 – I find out that my SAC is close to 10.8 l/min (which incidentally it is). For all further calculations, I know that now I can plug 11 l/min into my calculations and get results tailored pretty closely to my needs.

OK, now for all you folks who insist on sticking with American Customary Units, let's work through an example that will make sense to you.

First, you will need a baseline for the cylinder you choose to use. Unlike your metric buddy, the size of your cylinder tells you nothing directly about how many PSI equals a cubic foot of gas. And this is more or less what you need.

Actually, what you need, since SPGs are neither particularly accurate nor calibrated with fine gradations, is to know how many cubic feet are represented by a pressure drop of 100 psi.

To do this, you have to work out what's called a baseline for your cylinder. (Look at the chart on the next page for the baseline profiles of a few common cylinders.)

Tank nominal rated size	Rated pressure	Baseline cubic feet per 100 psi
Aluminum 80	3000 psi	2.6
Steel Faber FX117 (117 cft)	3442 psi	3.4
X-Series HP 100 Steel (99.5 cft)	3442 psi	2.9
LP-Series 95 Steel (93.3 cft)	2440 + (2640) psi	3.5
Aluminum 72	3000 psi	2.4
Aluminum 40	3000 psi	1.3

The simple method is to divide the cylinder's rated volume by its working pressure in units of 100 psi. For example, the rated volume of a Worthington X-Series 100 cubic foot steel cylinder has a rated volume of 100 cubic feet when filled to 3442 psi with gas at room temperature. (Its actual volume is slightly less, but no worries.) Therefore its baseline is found by dividing 100 by 34.42 = 2.9 which is often rounded to 3.0 for simplicity.

Therefore, 100 psi in that particular brand and model of cylinder is 3 cubic feet; 500 psi would be 15 cubic feet; 1000 psi would be 30 cubic feet; 3000 psi would be 90 and so on.

Obviously, the same pressure in two different cylinder makes and models usually represents a totally different volume of gas. For example, 1000 psi in a Faber 117 is around 34 cubic feet, but 1000 psi in an aluminum 72 is ten cubic feet less: i.e. only about 24 cubic feet.

Armed with an actual SAC, a diver can now calculate more precisely the gas volume needs for his dive, convert that volume from litres or cubic feet back into a pressure that can be read on his SPGs, and start to plan his dives.

A QUICK RECAP

There are many articles and books with excellent information about gas planning for technical dives, but just in case a refresher is called for, here are the Coles Notes on gas planning. This is an obviously important step for a staged decompression dive because a bolt to the surface is not practical; therefore running out of gas is not an option. But just as important, before the dive begins, the whole team must know how long the dive will be and how much of that time is going to be spent decompressing; and therefore what gases and how much will be needed to complete not just the dive but the decompression too.

We can use a 60 metre / 200 foot dive as an example. We'll start by working out how much gas we would need per minute at that depth. We will continue to use average SAC as the default, we will say that every diver in our team has the same consumption rate: 14 l/min or 0.5 cf/min. The table above shows that SAC adjusted to 98 l/min or 3.5 cf/min at depth. For a dive factor, we will use 1.5 (it not on the table but that's OK we'll use a calculator). So, we begin by knowing that at depth, each diver will consume 98 litres or 3.5 cubic feet every minute.

Let's get a sense for how long they can stay at depth. The major restriction on this dive will be gas volume. We will give each diver the same X-Series 100 Worthington steel tanks (two of them carried sidemount). This model is a 12 litre tank capable of being filled to 230 bar. The imperial equivalent makes it a 99 cubic foot tank at 3442 psi.

We must first find out what kind of fills everyone got from their dive shop. In our example, Diver A has 220 bar. Diver B has 3300 psi. Now, how much gas is that?

DIVER A:
Simply multiply 12 x 220 = 2640 litres. Diver A has two cylinders each with 2640 litres, which is a total gas volume of 5,280 litres.

DIVER B:
First has to work out the baseline for his tanks. That calculation is 99/34.42 = 2.87, which means every 100 psi equals 2.87 cubic feet.

He has 3300 psi in both tanks, therefore he has 33 x 2.87 = 94 cubic feet of gas in each tank and 188 cubic feet in both (rounded down slightly).

Question one: Is the controlling gas volume in Diver A's tanks or Diver B's? (Asking which has the controlling volume is the same as asking who has the least amount of gas. Usually both buddies would work in the same units of course, but regardless, the plan has to be constructed around the smallest volume.)

To find out, we will do a quick conversion and discover that 188 cubic feet equals 5,323 litres. Therefore, diver A has slightly less gas. Let's sense-check our results by converting diver A's 5280 litres into cubic feet. That gives us 186 cubic feet, so our first assumption was correct: Diver A has the least gas and hers is controlling volume.

Question two: Based on the controlling volume (5280 litres) how long can the team stay down? Well, at a consumption rate of 98 l/min, it will take 53 minutes to drain both tanks! Since we need to save at least a third of our gas for contingencies (like losing deco gas!), we have to knock at least one third off that time. The easiest way to do it is to multiply 53 minutes by 0.66, which will give us 35 minutes (66 percent or two thirds).

In addition, I would suggest a little extra contingency, so let's multiply by 60 percent rather than 66. The result of this slight change is a dive time of 32 minutes. Convention tells us that 32 minutes is our MAXIMUM bottom time and if our divers are as conservative as I believe them to be, they would cut tables for 22-25-28-32 minutes and aim for 25 or 28 minutes of bottom time.

(A quick note. An alternative method of finding the answer to the question: "How long can the team stay down?" we can use the controlling volume, put an extra few litres aside as an extra precaution, and use two-thirds of the remainder as the available gas. We then divide this figure by our estimated per minute consumption to arrive at a realistic guess for maximum bottom time.)

NEXT STEPS
Armed with a good estimate of the possible bottom times for a dive to 60 metres / 200 feet, our next steps would be to cut tables, work out our turn pressures for each diver, and figure out decompression gas needs.

Turn pressure is a cave-diving term that literally means: when the first diver's SPG shows this pressure, they have used half of their available gas (usually one-third of the starting or controlling volume) and it is time to turn-around and head back to "the exit."

In our example, we would have both turn pressure and turn time. Turn time would be approximately half of our target bottom time (or an elapsed time of about 13 minutes). Our turn pressure would be when a diver had used one-third of the pressure in each cylinder (minus the extra contingency gas) that represents one-third of the controlling volume.

Since we have a turn time and a maximum time already, there are a couple of ways to work out turn pressures (and apologies here but this is so much easier in metric units that I am going to work in them. The principles are the same for imperial but at this point, I am collecting spare change to buy Diver B SPGs in BAR).

We can simply say that our estimated turn time is 13 minutes. At 98 litres per minute, we will use 13 x 98 = 1274 litres. We have two 12 litre tanks to breathe those 1274 litres from, which is the same as one big 24 litre tank. Therefore 1294 / 24 = 54 bar. So our turn pressure is when the SPGs in both cylinders have dropped 54 bar.

Let's reverse engineer that figure. We started with 220 bar in each cylinder. One third of 220 bar is 73 bar (rounded down). Our turn pressure of 54 bar is way less (read conservative). Everything is fine. We have lots of contingency gas. We also know that when we reach our turn pressure or turn time, we have lots of leeway should something hit the fan, and on a 60 metre dive, that's a good risk management policy.

CCR BAILOUT

As I was working on this chapter, I ran into Jill Heinerth who told me that her new book will be about rebreather diving. I fully expect she will include a segment on calculations for bailout volumes, but I want to just touch on the topic here.

Bailout is gas that CCR divers carry with them in case their very expensive kit goes for a burton, and the diver has to revert to open-circuit to get back home. I usually carry a couple of bailout cylinders when deep diving or working in a cave. I have had incredible luck with my rebreathers not failing on me and I tend to drag the same bottle around with me for months before draining it and refilling. However, as unlikely as it seems that bailout will be used, I will always have it with me, even on short, shallow dives.

And that is the first point I wanted to make about CCR bailout: Always carry it.

The second point is lean towards redundancy. In an overhead, I carry two bottles as a minimum (unless of some special arrangement with stages and support divers), because open-circuit is prone to breaking. And it would be just my luck that the first time a rebreather turns belly up on me, my bailout's first stage will freeze.

The third point is volume. I have a resting SAC of 11 l/min yet I calculate my bailout needs at 30 l/min for the first five minutes (a DF of 2.7 in a bid to compensate for high rate of breathing following a CO_2 break-through), and 20 l/min (a DF of roughly 2.0) from there on. So what that means is if I am at 25 metres (3.5 bar), I will blow my way through 3.5 x 30 x 5 = 525 litres in the first five minutes while I get my act together. After that, for the rest of my swim at 25 metres (assuming a cave where I cannot start to head for the surface straight away), my consumption will drop to 3.5 x 20 = 70 l/min.

In truth, I have never tried to breathe that much gas and am unsure if I am capable of doing it. I may be way too conservative in my estimations. However, I've never met a diver who told me he had way too much gas when things went south, and as with the reassurance that comes from calculating a very comfy cushion to fall back on for an open-circuit dive to 60 metre / 200 foot dive, a lot of gas is just about enough.

STAGE BOTTLES

Which brings us to one final item: stage bottle gas management. Stages are the extra cylinders used to provide additional back gas, either for long cave penetrations or to conduct deep dives for extended periods.

With decompression bottles, we have a reasonably standard approach – work out how much you need, take twice that much – but the situation with stage bottles seems to be less standardized. The most often-asked question is: "Do I breathe one-third of the stage before switching or one-half… or something else?"

There really is no "Typical" application with stage bottles. The most common application is to use a stage or stages to extend a dive. A team will have primary cylinders, such as the X-Series tanks mentioned above, but will have a dive planned that is not possible using only the gas they hold. One or more stage bottles are called for. Typical deployment in a cave environment would see the team begin their dive breathing from their stage bottle. When the first team member has consumed one third of the controlling volume (same protocol used with primary gas and explained above), he or she signals other team members and, typically, stages the cylinder (drops it) someplace where it would be easy to find on the way back out. At that point, when only one stage is used, the whole team switches to back gas and continues.

This method – use one third and switch – is the most common conservative approach. An alternative – used typically in open water when stage bottles are used for the dive and the gas in one's primary cylinders is kept for emergencies (in other words, a diver will breathe from stage bottles for the whole dive: a tactic used when multiple dives are planned at a remote site). This second method is helpfully called: "half plus a bit" and

71

allows for a small reserve volume to be put aside – typically 300 litres or 10 cubic feet – and one half of the remaining volume is used before switching.

In practice, the difference between these two common methods is significant. Judge for yourself.

STAGE BOTTLE GAS VOLUME MANAGEMENT (COMPARISON)			
STARTING VOLUME 11 L ALUMINUM 80	USABLE VOLUME ONE THIRD METHOD	USABLE VOLUME HALF PLUS A BIT METHOD	DIFF. IN VOLUME/ TIME: AVERAGE SAC @ 4 BAR/ATA
2192 LITRES	660 LITRES	946 LITRES	286 litres 5 MINUTES OR LESS
77 CUBIC FEET	25 CUBIC FEET	33.5 CUBIC FEET	8.5 cubic feet 4.25 MINUTES OR LESS

LAST THOUGHT

Let's leave this topic with one last thought. As we were editing this chapter, I read about yet another incident where a diver "ran out of air." This time a pair of brothers and a friend were hunting crayfish in about 30 metres / 100 feet of water off the coast of New Zealand. Calm conditions at a site familiar to all three divers. According to reports based on the observations of his dive buddies, the victim did not pay attention to his consumption and was found dead on the bottom. Describing the unfortunate victim, his brother said: "He was a competent diver with several years' experience."

I would suggest an edit... a small change but something that I hope will speak volumes to you. "The victim was usually a competent diver, but not this time. Even several years' experience cannot compensate for serious oversight and inattention to the basics necessary for survival. He ignored the first rule of diving which requires all divers to always have something appropriate to breathe. He died because of it."

Plan your dive, dive your plan.

Chapter Five

GAS TOXICITY:
The transformation of gases at depth

Not having enough gas is a problem that manifests itself with determination and self-assurance. Running out of gas is immediately obvious to even the most inattentive open-circuit diver: suddenly, nothing to breathe! On the other hand, having the wrong gas is a problem with a fondness for secrecy and concealment. It may not make itself known to a diver until the damage is done: until it is too late to reverse the steep slide down to oblivion.

At the end of this chapter are a few tips to create your own management strategy. If you are pushed for time, you can skip right to it. If you do so and wonder about what, why, when, where, who and how, come back here and start to read.

Like so much that pertains to staying alive underwater, what folks don't know or don't understand the importance of, is what gets them and their buddies into trouble.

Gas toxicity is important because of the underhanded way it can create issues for us where no issues seem apparent. I have a couple of good friends to whom I no longer send birthday and Christmas cards because they ignored the basic guidelines for controlling and avoiding gas toxicity issues. It remains one issue that strongly governs the way I prepare for and execute my personal dives. And over the course of the next few pages, my goal is to underscore why I am such a nag about this issue.

Perhaps surprisingly, a diver does not have to venture very deep in the water column before breathing compressed gas opens him up to the potential of gas toxicity. This toxicity can take several forms: hyperoxia, hypoxia (and anoxia), hypercapnia, narcosis, and, in special cases, other toxins such as carbon monoxide poisoning. Even the air we breathe comfortably every day of our lives on dry land, goes through a Jekyll and Hyde transformation underwater.

INERT GAS NARCOSIS

For example, even in relatively shallow water – certainly no deeper than newly certified sport-divers are advised to dive – one of the side-effects from breathing compressed air is nitrogen narcosis. The effects of narcosis can begin to impair a diver's ability to "think fast and straight" within a few metres of the surface. Breathing normal compressed air at more extreme depths – and how deep that is depends on many factors besides the lineal distance to the surface – reaction times can slow dramatically, rational decision-making may be impaired, situational awareness can disappear. This behavior, while fine and even amusing in a clown at a kid's birthday party, can have devastating consequences underwater. Extreme reactions to nitrogen narcosis – sometimes tagged as inert gas narcosis – have been shown to turn a usually cautious and meticulous diver into someone who was a danger to himself and everyone diving with him.

However, that said, this type of severe reaction to the effects of narcosis is not guaranteed. Severe narcosis simply does not visit every diver who dives deep. Or, more accurately, it does not visit all divers to the same extent.

Every diver suffers some impairment, but individual divers react differently to that impairment. Also, for some, its effects increase gently and for others they arrive in a fire truck with the sirens blaring. Some report its effects as deep as 60 metres (200 feet) on air as "mild" while others would be comatose at that depth on that gas.

So, rather than generalise about its effect, we'd do better to understand that narcosis is not a monster that hangs around at a specific depth waiting to attack us. There is no red line at X-metres or Y-feet beyond which lay dragons and demons. The four horsemen of the apocalypse will not ride us down if we breathe air below some magical depth. Narcosis is not so easily pigeonholed.

Now that's not to say that one day, Pestilence, War, Famine, and Death will not suddenly appear out of the gloom approaching at a full gallop. That may indeed be in your stars if you dive deep on air or dive deep using any other gas. It's just that nobody can tell you the depth at which these visions will occur or indeed, if your reaction to extreme narcosis will instead cause you to chill out, see paisley fish, and start humming Grateful Dead tunes to yourself.

To complicate the issue even more, while I am unaware of any hard-edged physiological studies that are able to explain why the character of narcosis presents can be benign one day and cruel the next, but this certainly is the case. I have witnessed a diver who was perfectly comfortable working with a specific narcotic loading one day, act like a character from Monty Python's Flying Circus at the same depth and narcotic load a few days later.

This incident and others like it, lend credence to the suggestion that there is far more at work than a simple lineal relationship between nitrogen partial pressure and the effects of narcosis.

OTHER FACTORS

Among the factors that are thought to contribute to the rapidity of onset, and the severity of narcosis are:

- Increased partial pressures of CO_2 (the result of hard work, swimming against a current, working with camera equipment, skip-breathing, etc.)
- Thermal Stress (being cold at depth)
- Being drunk or diving with a hangover or diving under the influence of "recreational" drugs
- Diving tired or after a poor night's sleep (which is a type of fatigue many poor sailors suffer on live-aboard vacations)
- High WOB (work of breathing) related to the breathing resistance within the system being used (whether open-circuit, semi-closed circuit or closed-circuit)
- Anxiety or apprehension: including ironically, irrational fear of nitrogen narcosis
- Side-effects from various prescription and over-the-counter medications (motion sickness meds for example)
- Rapid descent (especially when coupled with the following…)
- Vertigo or temporary disorientation caused by the diver having no 'up' reference such as in clear 'blue water' or in water with very poor visibility
- Task-loading stress (unfamiliarity with equipment, buddy, environment et al.)
- Temporal stress (feeling rushed and under pressure to accomplish a task)
- Diving with a cold or flu, especially if medicated
- Increased oxygen partial pressure (see below)

ADAPTION

Adaptation to narcosis is a rather controversial sub-topic. Some experienced divers suggest that with practice and experience, and with the help of some simple breathing and preparatory techniques, the effects of narcosis can be controlled. The degree of control is specific to individuals, and tolerances to narcosis can vary from day to day: but many experienced deep divers will tell you that "adaptation" to narcosis does take place.

In his book on diving medicine, Peter Bennett, founder of DAN (Diver's Alert Network) and currently the Senior Director of the Center for Hyperbaric Medicine and

Environmental Physiology at Duke University Medical Centre, wrote: "the novice diver may expect to be relatively seriously affected by nitrogen narcosis, but subjectively at least there will be improvement with experience. Frequency of exposure [to narcosis] does seem to result in some level of adaptation."

The actual mechanics of adaptation are neither completely understood nor proven but there is a consensus among a segment of experienced deep divers who agree that the effects of narcosis seem to lessen with repeated, progressively deeper exposures.

Bret Gilliam, while writing on the topic in an article for Diver Magazine, stated:

"For the diver who regularly faces deep exposures, a tolerance far in excess of the unadapted diver will be exhibited. A gradual work-up to increasing depths is the best recommendation. I refer to making each first dive of the day progressively deeper than the day before to build tolerances, i.e. Day one: first dive to 150 feet, Day two: first dive to 175 feet etc. Subsequent dives on Day one and Day two would be shallower than the first. This process should be over several days' time if the diver has been away from deep diving for more than two weeks. Adaptation appears to be lost exponentially as acquired so no immediate increased narcosis susceptibility will necessarily be evident but divers are cautioned to exercise great conservatism if any lay-off is necessitated."

Gilliam, a pioneering technical diver whose 40-year career in the sport includes founding Technical Diving International and registering a world-record deep dive on air to 145 metres (475 feet) in 1993, is surprisingly circumspect about deep-air diving.

"I would like to emphasize that deep air diving below 218 feet [slightly deeper than 66 metres] is generally not recommended given the alternatives available in today's industry. This depth represents the outer limits of recommended oxygen exposures at 1.6 ATA of oxygen.

For high risk or particularly demanding dives this depth should be adjusted shallower. Many veteran air divers now opt for mixed gas that virtually eliminates narcosis and oxygen toxicity problems."

SYMPTOMS

However well one may tolerate narcosis, and in spite of conditioning and experience, eventually, it influences the performance of all divers. It should be added that even when breathing gases containing copious amounts of helium as a strategy to reduce narcosis, some level of impairment must always be assumed when diving. The classic textbook symptoms of narcosis are light-headedness, slowed reflexes, euphoria, reduction of peripheral vision, localized numbness or tingling, and difficulty making decisions (euphemistically called cotton-wool head).

Individuals who recognise that all dives are conducted under some narcotic loading – and who have prepared themselves to dive deep – constantly monitor themselves for more subtle signs that signal things are beginning to slide. These early symptoms often start with difficulty reading gauges, especially the finer graduations on depth and pressure gauges. Sounds begin to distort and become somewhat louder. Time seems to pass more slowly… or more quickly. Perceptual narrowing adds a degree of added complexity to the operation of basic equipment such as clips, buttons and switches.

An experienced diver can learn to control these deficiencies and work within them, but these shifts in perception can present real danger and cannot be underestimated. Gilliam's advice notwithstanding, we would do well to make no assumptions that what was fine at depth "Y" yesterday will be acceptable at the same depth today. Getting chilled during pre-dive preparations, feeling the effects of a poor night's sleep etc. can result in dangerous oversight. Self-monitoring and stress-assessment are critical skills before and during a dive. A diver at 60 metres with a poor perception of time and depth, as well as confusion about the location of a safe exit and remaining gas volume, has a diminished chance of survival.

What follows is a list of symptoms. Your mileage may vary but learning these and being on the lookout for them, may help you avoid a brush with the four horsemen.

- Light-headedness
- Euphoria
- Impaired neuromuscular coordination
- Hearing sensitivity or hallucination
- Slowed mental activity
- Decreased problem solving capacity
- Overconfidence
- Short-term memory loss
- Improper time perceptions
- Inability to focus on fine work
- Exaggerated movements
- Numbness and tingling in lips, face and feet
- Stupor and a sense of carelessness
- Sense of impending blackout
- Levity or tendency to laughter
- Depressive state
- Visual hallucination or disturbances
- Perceptual narrowing

- Less tolerance to stress
- Exaggerated (oversized) handwriting
- Amnesia
- Loss of consciousness
- Retardation of higher mental processes
- Retardation of task performances
- Slurred speech
- Poor judgment
- Slowed reaction time and reflex ability
- Loss of mechanical dexterity

YET ANOTHER INFLUENCE ON NARCOSIS... PERHAPS

In addition to the effects and influences of an elevated nitrogen partial pressure, cold, workload, stress et al., on a diver's perceptions and performance at depth, there is the issue/controversy surrounding oxygen narcosis: or more correctly, the debate over whether oxygen is or is not also narcotic.

This particular question seems no closer to being resolved as I write this than it was a couple of decades ago when some fledgling technical diver first posed the question.

David Sawatzky is a very experienced technical diver, a member of the advisory board for a major training agency, and a medical doctor whose resume includes spells doing research into diving physiology for the Canadian military.

In the late 1990s, he published an article on the topic of oxygen narcosis in which he stated: "The scientific data available do NOT support the conclusion that oxygen is narcotic. They also do not and cannot show that oxygen has no narcotic effect. Oxygen might somehow be involved in the entire question of narcosis and [diver] performance but it is clearly not more narcotic than nitrogen. The narcotic gases are all chemically inert in the body. In contrast, oxygen is one of the most chemically active substances in nature."

A Hollis DC7 first stage with 500 SE side-exhaust second. A modern high-performance regulator solution for deep mix diving in tough conditions.

After reading Dr. Sawatzky's article, and after private conversations with him and other medical doctors who've research the subject, plus interviews with many professional and non-professional divers, and 25 years' experience conducting dives using nitrox, pure oxygen, trimix, heliox and a couple of more exotic gases myself, what I hear is this. If you are looking for scientific evidence about oxygen narcosis and how it may or may not add to the effects of nitrogen narcosis, you are going to be hard-pressed.

It seems difficult to measure the influence of oxygen with any quantitative accuracy at this date. This may change but as it stands, since a change cannot be measured, in practical terms, oxygen narcosis either is not there or is too small to matter.

Frankly, as interesting as the debate over oxygen narcosis may be, I believe deep divers have other oxygen toxicity concerns on which to focus.

HYPEROXIA and OXYGEN TOXICITY

Hyperoxia means "more oxygen" and a hyperoxic gas simply contains more oxygen than normal air. When divers speak of hyperoxic gas or hyperoxic mixes, chances are they are talking about nitrox.

Nitrox, is a blend of oxygen and air first introduced to recreational divers by Dick Rutkowski, and is hyperoxic because it contains a higher fraction of oxygen than the approximately 21 percent found in air. The fraction of oxygen in nitrox can be anything from 22 percent to 99 percent.

Rutkowski, the former deputy diving safety officer with the National Oceanic and Atmospheric Administration (NOAA), later formed IAND (International Association of Nitrox Divers) and began teaching nitrox use to civilian recreational divers in 1985. At that time, he reasoned that the benefits of diving with nitrox enjoyed by divers at NOAA – more bottom-time, shorter surface intervals, and fewer incidents of DCS – would also be of considerable benefit to recreational divers. Many old-school dive instructors considered Rutkowski's actions dangerous, and assurances that Nitrox was appropriate for regular divers like you and me, were met with heavy skepticism.

Initially, agencies such as PADI and BSAC refused to sanction nitrox training or even nitrox use. But of course, attitudes change and, to quote Rutkowski himself: "Science Always Wins Over Bullshit." After a decade or so, common-sense prevailed to the point where today every major certifying agency offers nitrox training on somewhat similar lines to the curriculum originally presented by Rutkowski.

Indeed, nitrox has become so established that certification in its use is sometimes offered as an acceptable adjunct to basic open-water training. You would think therefore that there is little to be discussed concerning what nitrox is, how to dive with it, and what to be careful of when mixing, carrying and breathing it. I am dismayed to say that this does not appear to be the case. An alarming proportion of divers certified in its use and even instructors "teaching" others how to use nitrox, seem to have lost sight of several important objectives or principles. Let's deal with a couple of them here.

LET'S RECAP NITROX BASICS

In diving, hyperoxic gases deliver greater oxygen partial pressures to a diver than air at the same depth, and when divers breathe hyperoxic gases at greater than normal atmospheric pressure – for example when they are underwater – there is a chance of running afoul of something called oxygen toxicity.

Specifically, the type of oxygen toxicity that divers need to be aware of affects their central nervous system, and is called central nervous system or CNS toxicity. It is a result of breathing extremely high oxygen partial pressures for relatively short periods of time.

This of course, is exactly the situation when a diver breathes nitrox at depth, and many authorities, including NOAA, suggest that any gas carries some potential for CNS toxicity if it delivers a partial pressure of oxygen (ppO2) that is above 0.6 atmospheres at depth!

CNS is not the only form of oxygen toxicity, and we'll touch on others later in this chapter, but it is the potential effects of oxygen on the central nervous system that demands divers keep track of their exposure to oxygen and their proximity to well-established limits for CNS loading. This is key to avoiding CNS issues.

It is essential for a diver using hyperoxic gases to understand that the likelihood of a tonic-clonic type seizure while underwater increases as his exposure to hyperbaric oxygen increases.

Quite obviously, having a seizure-type event of any kind while diving can turn a diver into a statistic. The seizure itself is not mortal, but the predictable outcome of a seizure underwater is drowning, embolism or heart attack: in short, the victim usually dies.

The extent of a diver's oxygen exposure is a function of oxygen partial pressure (sometimes referred to as oxygen DEPTH), coupled with TIME at that depth.

As the oxygen partial pressure being delivered by a gas increases, the shorter time the diver can spend breathing that gas before the safe limits of his exposure will be reached. These two factors combined indicate the OXYGEN DOSE or CNS LOADING.

Luckily for those of us who want to derive the physiological benefits that nitrox offers (and let's assume we do and work through the process), tracking CNS exposure is relatively simple, thanks to Dick Rutkowski's old employer: NOAA.

When Rutkowski began teaching the use of nitrox to recreational divers, he had a very solid grounding in the pros and cons of diving hyperoxic gases. The divers he had overseen while at NOAA breathed oxygen enriched gases to conduct their underwater research. NOAA sanctioned the general use of nitrox for shallow dives, and the organization had developed simple operating procedures and special tables to help keep its divers healthy and whole, and its operations safe from the threat of CNS oxygen toxicity.

Today, more than a quarter of a century later, NOAA's Tables have become the gold standard. They have been adopted as such and are used unaltered by most agencies who certify divers in nitrox use. The tables themselves are also simple to read: perhaps among the most straightforward of any employed in the realm of diving. However, before they can be of use, we have to do a take a couple of preliminary steps. We must also be cautious that when we when we plug into our dive plan the advice they give us, we completely understand the implications and scope of that advice.

MANAGING CNS: A SIMPLE EXAMPLE

The first concept we need to grasp if we're to safely manage CNS toxicity is that oxygen partial pressure represents just one factor of our total oxygen dose. The tables give us readings for oxygen partial pressures from a maximum recommended level of 1.6 bar to 0.6 bar.

We already understand that the value for oxygen partial pressure is specific to the percentage of oxygen in our breathing gas and the depth at which we intend to breathe it. Take for example, a gas that has been tested with an oxygen analyser and which contains 31 percent oxygen.

From a quick glance at NOAA's tables (see page 96) we can see that the maximum value for the ppO2 from any gas is 1.6 bar. When a gas such as nitrox is at a depth that results in a ppO2 of 1.6 bar it is said to be at its Maximum Operating Depth or MOD. A modified MOD for a gas may be calculated when it delivers less than 1.6 bar (1.4 or 1.3 bar for example) but the absolute maximum depth at 1.6 bar should never be exceeded.

To calculate the MOD of a gas, we divide the target ppO2 by the fraction of oxygen the gas contains – which results in a value for the depth expressed in ambient pressure – and then subtract one and move the decimal place one digit to the right. It sounds more complicated than it is.

Here are the MOD calculations for two gases at opposite ends of the gas spectrum. Pure oxygen has an MOD of 1.6 (maximum acceptable ppO2) divided by 100, which is the percentage of oxygen in the mix. The answer to that simple calculation is 1.60 bar. This is the ambient pressure at which oxygen is at its MOD. To change that ambient pressure to metres, subtract 1 and move the decimal. Therefore the MOD of pure oxygen is 6 metres. The MOD for air is 1.6/0.21 which equals an ambient pressure of 7.61 bar. To change that to a depth in metres, subtract one (6.61) and move the decimal. Doing so, we arrive at the MOD of air which is 66.1 metres.

The ppO2 of 1.6 bar has been adopted as the top-end limit by just about every member of the diving community including the technical training agencies. Most open-circuit technical divers will opt to breathe a gas delivering this ppO2 briefly during staged decompression. This action, as part of a complete dive where other gases are employed, requires careful planning and following established procedures, but it is "normal" in that application. On many closed-circuit rebreathers, an oxygen partial pressure of just a knat's hair more than 1.6 bar will trigger visual and/or audible alarms. So, since 1.6 bar is the maximum ppO2 acceptable for ANY gas, we need to find out if the nitrox with 31 percent oxygen in it will deliver less than or more than this at the deepest planned depth for our dive.

Oxygen Partial Pressure and Normal Exposure Time Limits for working dives (NOAA 1991 Diving Manual)		
Oxygen Partial Pressure Bar or ATA	Maximum Duration (mins.) Single Dive	Maximum Total Duration (mins.) 24-hour period
1.6	45	150
1.5	120	180
1.4	150	180
1.3	180	210
1.2	210	240
1.1	240	270
1.0	300	300
0.9	360	360
0.8	450	450
0.7	570	570
0.6	720	720

N.B. Plan CNS exposures of no more than 80 percent of NOAA's published limits.

For the sake of a simple example, let's work with a dive planned to 35 metres. To discover, what oxygen partial pressure a gas containing 31 percent oxygen delivers to the diver breathing it at 35 metres, we need first to know what the ambient pressure is at that "target depth." The metric system makes this sort of calculation very easy.

We simply move the decimal point one number to the left and add one to the whole number. In other words, the ambient pressure at 35 metres is 4.5 bar. (If you are using imperial units, the process is to divide the depth in feet by 33 (the number of feet of salt water that represents an increase of one atmosphere of pressure) and add one to the answer.

A diver using American Customary Units will encounter an ambient pressure of 4.5 ata at about 115 feet.

Using Dalton's Gas Law, we find the oxygen partial pressure of a gas by multiplying together the ambient pressure at target depth by the fraction of oxygen in that gas. In this case: 4.5 x 0.31 which equals 1.4; and the NOAA tables inform us that this ppO2 is within useable range.

For a ppO2 of 1.4 bar, the tables show two oxygen time limits: 150 minutes maximum duration for a single dive, and 180 minutes maximum duration for daily exposure. We need to track both.

In simple terms, if our dive to 35 metres comprised 20 minutes of bottom-time (pushing the no-decompression limits a little), we would have used a trifle more than 13 percent of our allowable single dive limit – perfectly within reason – and approximately 11 percent of our daily allotment.

Clearly, this dive presents little menace of CNS toxicity for a single dive, and it would require us to conduct nine similar dives in a day to approach the daily limit! We might also add that since the MOD of an EAN31 (nitrox with 31 percent oxygen) is 41.6 metres, more than six metres deeper than we intend to dive, our dive will be within the no decompression limit (NDL) for a normal sport dive.

However, technical dives are frequently conducted beyond the limits of no-decompression. In these special cases CNS limits can easily be approached and exceeded by the unwary.

It is also considered very dangerous to exceed the MOD for a specific gas since CNS loading above 1.6 bar follows an exponential curve, such that the maximum allowable time drops dramatically.

THE IMPORTANCE OF TIME
Of course, if a non-technical diver were in the habit of pushing limits, he too might run into CNS troubles. For example, to operate any flavor of nitrox safely, it's necessary to understand what those top and bottom-end partial pressures on the NOAA tables actually represent.

For example, without reference to time, diving with a ppO2 of 1.6 is no more dangerous and no safer than using one delivering 1.4 or 1.2 bar. During decompression dives, most experienced technical divers have no hesitation breathing a gas that delivers 1.6 bar of oxygen for several minutes.

Most informed nitrox users understand that their CNS loading after this short-duration blast of oxygen at 1.6 bar would be less likely to result in CNS toxicity than spending three hours sucking back a gas delivering 1.4 bar, since the maximum time limit for a gas at 1.4 bar is only two and a half hours.

The important missing information in many conversations about diving nitrox – especially in onLine dive forums – is time. When making an informed decision whether or not a particular partial pressure is safe to breathe, the critical question to ask is: "How long will I be breathing it for?"

For example, there are circumstances under which it would be perfectly fine for a properly-trained sport diver to plan a 25-minute dive on using a gas that delivers a ppO2 of 1.6 bar. The CNS loading afterwards would be the bottom-time expressed as a fraction of the total allowable time. In this case 25 minutes divided by 45 minutes, which equals a little more than 55.5 percent of the allowable dose.

There is no more danger with a 55.5 percent exposure to oxygen at 1.6 than there is with a 55.5 percent exposure at 1.4 or 1.3. The resulting oxygen dose is exactly the same; and it is the total dose, not the ppO2, which determines one's risk factor.

What does add somewhat to the risk of diving a gas delivering a ppO2 of 1.6 bar is that any loss of position in the water column through either poor buoyancy control or inattention, very rapidly eats up "allowable" oxygen time. Because of this and other considerations such as currents, cold, workload and related stressors, experienced divers seldom operate with oxygen partial pressures above 1.4 bar for bottom mix.

24-HOUR CNS LIMITS
NOAA's 24-hour CNS limits seem to have many divers bewildered: some instructors too. I have had friends who'd taught technical programs for years, confess they did not understand how the daily limits work!

What's baffling is there's really very little to understand. Perhaps what's confused people is the higher-profile but much more complicated suggestion based on NOAA's single-dive limits that CNS loading has a 90-minute half-time.

In other words, some divers believe that if a diver surfaces with a CNS loading of X percent, after 90 minutes on the surface that loading will have dropped to ½X percent.

This is not a technique suggested or recommended in any NOAA manual that I know of and was characterized as "poor science" by Dr. Bill Hamilton.

The only CNS loading tied to a 90-minute half-time in NOAA publications are exposures delivering an oxygen partial pressure of 1.6 bar / ata. These are the ONLY exposures given a half-time of any sort.

If we check out the single dive limit for 1.6 bar (45 minutes) and compare it to the daily limit (150 minutes), it becomes apparent something different goes on compared to what happens with lesser ppO2s.

I have heard it said that NOAA daily limits are a proxy for pulmonary toxicity management. They are not. This is complete nonsense.

Pulmonary toxicity has nothing to do with these calculations or the need to be vigilant keeping tabs on 24-hour CNS toxicity limits.

It is true that if one keeps within CNS limits (both single dive and 24-hour) the chances of classic pulmonary toxicity are extremely unlikely, but there should be no confusion between the two.

Daily CNS limits can become an issue when multiple dives are planned and is particularly important for divers doing Live-Aboard trips where the first dive of day two can easily be less than 12 hours after the last dive of day one!

Here's an example of how easily the 24-hour limit can be reached in this kind of multi-dive, multi-day scenario.

One arrival at the first dive site on Monday, our enthusiastic diver conducts a dive starting at 20:00 it will earn him a 20 percent CNS exposure when he surfaces some time later. On Tuesday morning, day two, at 09:00 he does a second dive that also racks up 20 percent exposure. At noon, 12:00, his third dive nets 25 percent; and the series wraps up at 15:00 with a fourth dive that also earns 25 percent CNS loading. So, the total CNS loading for his first four dives adds up to 90 percent (20 + 20 + 25 + 25 = 90).

One minute and 24 hours after surfacing from this first dive, his CNS loading (according to the NOAA tables) will have shed the 20 percent earned in his Monday evening dive. He will be clear to dive, but must be wary of the potential CNS loading from what will be the fifth dive in the series. He has 30 percent "available" to him (10 percent remainder plus 20 percent credit from the first dive more than 24 hours prior).

REACHING 24-HOUR LIMITS

He can do a fifth dive but should be aware that NOAA recommends that if the 24-hour limit is reached, he should stay out of the water for 24 hours. Furthermore, some divers stay out of the water for 12 hours if their daily CNS load exceeds 80 percent of the 24-hour limit (which he reached at the end of his fourth dive).

Many divers believe that when they do pure sport diving within recreational limits, it's hard to exceed the daily limits. It is not. The examples used here are not extraordinary exposures for a sport diver. Many "normal" resort or live-aboard dives could earn a diver 20 percent or 25 percent of their daily allowance.

Consider the NOAA daily limit for dives at 1.4 bar ppO2 (the norm for many operations). It is 180 minutes. Twenty percent of that is only 36 minutes! Four 36-minute dives in a day are not unusual for an active diver on a multi-day diving vacation where the water is warm and nitrox is available.

Given the potential consequences, it seems worth the effort to keep track of 24-hour limits. Unfortunately few personal dive computers seem to track 24-hour limits in spite of several instances of technical divers suffering CNS episodes.

And speaking of technical divers, the situation for them, can be far more compelling.

Although some technical divers insist on using the half-time approach. I believe following NOAA's recommendations is easier, and at very least is backed up by some data and actual dives.

It may make things any easier, if we think of the body's capacity to deal with CNS loading as a bucket sitting on the ground. In both the half-time and 24-hour models, water is added to and taken from the bucket every time we dive. The half-time model describes a leak, and in the 24-hour model uses a ladle is used to remove water. Bill Hamilton, who worked on the NOAA limits and recommendations, saw CNS exposure over multiple dives/days as a bucket and ladle model.

Water flows into the bucket from a spigot that represents dive loading. In the live-aboard example above, at the finish of dive 4 (a dive that began at 15:00 on Tuesday), the bucket is 80 percent full. At 20:36 on Tuesday, a magic ladle dips into the water and removes 20 percent of its contents. Yes, the diver can dive again, but a dive netting more than a 30 percent loading means the bucket will overflow. Potentially making the floor wet and ruining his or her day.

As with so much that deals with physiology, there are many, many variables at play with CNS toxicity. NOAA's guidelines are based on data collected from NOAA divers on working dives, and wet and dry chamber runs. I understand that having a bucket and magic ladle is worrisome, but the model works and has worked in the recreational arena since the mid-1980s, so it's what we have to work with by default and best practice. Is it logical? Of course not. It's physiology and there is little logic involved with the workings of the human body. Exceptions are the norm.

What Hamilton was striving for by including 24-hour limits in the NOAA tables was a simple system that was workable and 'safe.' His concern (shared by a lot of experienced technical divers) is that CNS has too many variables to be taken lightly. Track CNS and stay clear of the prescribed limits: well clear.

ANOTHER FORM OF OXYGEN TOXICITY

Just when you begin to feel comfortable with your understanding of oxygen toxicity, some idiot comes along and muddies the water. Allow me to be the first to wade around in your comfort zone kicking up silt.

Breathing higher than normal ppO2 over very long periods of time, can result in whole body or pulmonary intoxication. This condition – very different to CNS toxicity – is more correctly called the Lorrain-Smith effect. James Lorrain Smith, a Scottish pathologist working on respiration at the turn of the 20th century, researched and identified the condition first.

Pulmonary toxicity can occur with exposure to partial pressures of oxygen greater than 0.5 bar. The signs and symptoms are inflammation of the throat and upper airways, a burning sensation in the chest, and shortness of breath. Lorrain-Smith does not result in seizure and is really not an issue for the vast majority of divers. It CAN manifest itself in as few as four hours breathing a ppO2 of as little as 0.8 bar but most textbooks seem to peg a time of 12-14 hours as the norm for symptoms to manifest at this level of oxygen.

There are few if any documented cases of recreational sport divers suffering from Lorrain-Smith toxicity. When nitrox courses were first designed – and remember nitrox was only offered by "technical" agencies at this time – ALL divers were asked to keep track of pulmonary loading, and were introduced to Oxygen Toxicity Units (OTUs).

The formula used to calculate this pulmonary exposure to oxygen looked like this:
$$OTU = T_x \left(0.5/(ppO2-0.5)\right)^{-0.833}$$

Yes, that is an exponential number stuck there at the end. Get out your scientific calculators. And to those reading this who do not own a scientific calculator and whose facial expression now resembles that of a bulldog chewing a wasp: you are not alone.

Those of us charged to write or edit student materials at that time, very quickly learned from massive quantities of customer feedback, that few divers, the majority of whom we can safely assume were successful, functioning members of their communities with steady jobs and smoothly running businesses, remembered how to use the exponent function on a scientific calculator: if indeed they were ever asked to learn how.

The second edition of many nitrox manuals therefore also contained a table that was designed to make the whole OTU tracking process much more user-friendly. One simply found one's oxygen partial pressure in one column and read from left to right to find a corresponding value (OTUs per minute of exposure) in the next column.

For example, for the sample dive used earlier, 20 minutes at 1.4 bar, the diver would accumulate 20 times 1.631 OTUs: or about 32 or 33 oxygen toxicity units. The question of course is: Exactly what does that mean?

Well, for a single-day exposure, a dose of 850 OTUs is said to reduce vital capacity – which is the term to describe a person's ability to fill their lungs – by four percent. Most diving textbooks that talk at all about pulmonary toxicity suggest a daily limit of 300 OTUs for multiple dives over multiple days.

Table for Calculating Pulmonary Toxicity	
Oxygen Partial Pressure	OTU per minute
0.6 BAR	0.262
0.7 BAR	0.466
0.8 BAR	0653
0.9 BAR	0.830
1.0 BAR	1.000
1.1 BAR	1.164
1.2 BAR	1.323
1.3 BAR	1.479
1.4 BAR	1.631
1.5 BAR	1.781
1.6 BAR	1.928

Clearly, to reach 300 OTUs and run the risk of suffering from Lorrain-Smith toxicity, a diver would have to be breathing ppO2s high enough and long enough to put him or her well beyond the acceptable CNS limit. (As an example, to accumulate 300 OTUs a diver would have to breathe oxygen at 6 metres or 20 feet for a trifle longer than three hours. Clearly, this type of exposure is outside the purview of anything but extreme technical diving and should have the reader asking: "Wouldn't that type of exposure open the diver up to a CNS incident?" Which of course, it probably would.

In part, because for most dives and the vast majority of divers, pulmonary or whole body concerns seem mote, third and later editions of basic nitrox texts dropped both the equation and table and instead usually contained a short reference to Lorrain Smith at most.

For most of us, recreational as well as technical divers, it is always CNS that offers the real threat. As long as we keep within the limits of CNS toxicity, pulmonary toxicity can be ignored, and in my experience, the majority of technical divers do not bother to track their status for pulmonary toxicity.

But this attitude does seem to have led to confusion. For example, PADI's DSAT tech deep manual contains the advice: *"The CNS clock also manages pulmonary oxygen toxicity."*

This well-meaning but poorly worded advice has begat a whole community of divers and instructors who believe that OTUs are another way to track CNS toxicity. They are not. OTUs have nothing to do with CNS and one cannot interchange one measurement of oxygen exposure to manage the other. For example, there is a strong likelihood that if a diver were to use OTUs to track her CNS oxygen exposure, she would become a statistic. CNS and pulmonary oxygen toxicity are NOT the same thing, and OTUs track ONLY pulmonary toxicity.

One last note on this topic. The gases used to mix decompression gases have a high percentage of oxygen and oxygen is supplied to mixing stations with very little humidity (a dew-point of minus 40 is common). Consequently, decompression gases, indeed all OC breathing gases, require the diver add water vapor as they travel to his or her lungs. This, coupled with having to warm gases to a temperature acceptable in the body, taxes divers.

After a long dive, many technical divers complain of pulmonary-like symptoms, yet their oxygen exposure is too light for classic Lorrain Smith toxicity to be the culprit. Many believe that in these cases, individuals are suffering from "dry-air asthma." Perhaps the special circumstances that technical divers find themselves in need to be identified by a new "syndrome" or perhaps we can simply broaden the definition of mild pulmonary toxicity to include this effect. Not a very scientific approach may be but it would not be the first time science has been bent to accommodate the needs and demands of recreational diving.

HYPOXIA, HYPERCAPNIA, CARBON MONOXIDE

We have touched on the basic issues of Narcosis and Hyperoxia, now let's move on to the evil triplets: hypoxia, hypercapnia, and carbon monoxide poisoning. Each of these topics will make appearances in later chapters, but we can spend a few minutes now making sure we understand what each term describes and the simplest ways to avoid the consequences of each.

Hypoxia (technically the term is hypoxic hypoxia) describes a condition in which there is too little oxygen getting to a diver's lungs. Climbers, kids breathing from helium balloons, and CCR divers are all have a strong potential to suffer the results of hypoxia, and certainly there are several protocols and procedures aimed at keeping the last group in that list safe.

Hypoxia has such potentially devastating results that these protocols are drilled into new CCR divers even before they are "allowed" to breath from a rebreather on dry land let alone underwater. However, ALL divers need to be aware of the situations where the gas they are breathing will not support consciousness.

The most common threat to OC divers (open-circuit or divers using traditional scuba gear), is breathing from a hypoxic mix at a depth where that mix does not deliver an oxygen partial pressure very close to "Normoxic:" that's to say, a ppO2 of 0.20 bar.

Different certification agencies each set very slightly different limits to the fraction of oxygen that is acceptable for divers to breathe on the surface. My personal comfort zone on OC restricts me to an absolute minimum ppO2 of 0.18 bar.

A gas containing 18 percent of oxygen will deliver approximately that ppO2 at sea level, and of course the partial pressure would drop if we took that cylinder into the mountains – or any place where the atmospheric pressure drops below 101 kilopascals – and it would increase if we took it underwater.

There is a general consensus concerning various "low-end" oxygen exposure limits: 0.10 bar is the point at which people will pass out and eventually die. At a ppO2 of approximately 0.14 bar, hypoxia symptoms such as cyanosis, headache, slow reaction time, impaired judgment, euphoria, visual impairment or loss of acuity, drowsiness, light-headedness or dizziness, tingling in fingers and toes, and general numbness may be felt.

The minimum ppO2 that allows normal function in "most people" is 0.16 bar, but even moderate exertion (put surface swimming in scuba gear in that category) may cause hypoxia. The author can swim, skip and jump at a ppO2 of 0.18 bar, that's why it is my benchmark. Normoxic is said to be a ppO2 between 0.20 and 0.21. It's even safer.

A real potential for an hypoxic incident exists when gases for extremely deep dives are being prepared for use. I've found that the best practice is to make sure cylinders containing ANY gas with an oxygen contents of less than 18 percent are clearly marked: DO NOT BREATHE. HYPOXIC GAS. Also, NEVER leave a regulator attached to an unattended bottle containing hypoxic mix.

The best, most effective and simplest ways to avoid hypoxia for divers and for people handling or simply hanging around scuba cylinders is to analyse ALL gases, label cylinders clearly, and to store cylinders out of reach of children.

Hypercapnia means "too much" carbon dioxide. The circumstances under which an OC diver would run into problems associated with too much carbon dioxide (called CO_2 poisoning in some dive communities), would be:

- breathing from a poorly designed or irregularly serviced regulator
- over-breathing due to a high work rate (swimming against a strong current, swimming hard with camera equipment, etc.)
- improper use of gear with dead space (a full-face mask for example)
- high work of breathing due to gas density (breathing air at great depth for example)
- lack of aerobic fitness
- skip breathing.

Among the symptoms and signs of hypercapnia are flushed skin, rapid breathing (tachypnea), a feeling of air starvation (dyspnea), irregular or skipped heartbeat, muscle twitches, jerky movements, and a rise in blood pressure. Mild hypercapnia, for example when a diver constantly tries to skip breathe, can cause headache, confusion and lethargy.

Normal levels of CO_2 in atmospheric air are between 0.036 percent (360 parts per million) and 0.040 percent (400 parts per million). Levels might be considerably higher in a poorly ventilated space, but unless things have gone seriously wrong, or someone is sitting with a plastic bag over their head, it's unlikely anyone on the surface in normal circumstances will run into the higher levels that are possible when diving: and particularly when diving a rebreather.

Severe hypercapnia, symptoms can rapidly progress to disorientation and panic, convulsions, unconsciousness and eventually lead to death.

Closed-circuit divers have to be particularly careful to avoid CO_2 poisoning, but in open-circuit diving too, its symptoms need to be recognized and conditions that may result in it should be avoided.

Some rebreather manufacturers have managed to overcome the technical challenges presented by detecting CO2 in a damp environment with constantly changing gas density, and now manufacture and sell working CO2 sensor systems on several different models of CCR.

At this point, these sensors detect the presence of CO2 at the head of the scrubber (a spot where zero carbon dioxide is the norm). The system I am most familiar with is made by Ambient Pressure Diving out of the UK and has been designed to work with that company's Inspiration, Evolution and Evolution+ CCRs running its proprietary Vision Software.

The AP sensor is an active warning device using infrared technology to "read" for CO2 and when activated warns the diver that the CO2 content of his or her breathing gas is approaching a dangerous level. (This could be due to depletion of the Sofnolime, incorrect assembly, or extremely hard work.) Since the sensor's introduction in 2013, the company has sold hundreds of the systems so the peace of mind from this type of monitor obviously strikes rebreather divers as a worthwhile idea. The AP CO2 sensor is intended as an option that can be used with or without the company's Temp Stick Scrubber monitor.

Carbon monoxide (CO) is a highly toxic gas that is a by-product of incomplete combustion. It presents a serious threat to everyone because it bonds more readily than oxygen does with hemoglobin (the protein in red blood cells that transports oxygen around our body). It's a special concern to divers since it's produced by gasoline-powered engines, and even very small quantities of engine exhaust being sucked into a compressor's air intact can easily cause poisoning at depth. Also, the compressor itself if not monitored and serviced regularly is capable of producing levels of the gas well above trace quantities with no outside influences at all.

Most compressors use hydrocarbon lubricating oil and if seals around the pistons are worn or damaged, traces of these oils may be drawn into the compressor's cylinder and ignited during compression.

Something similar may happen when the filters in a compressor fail and dust and other organic particulate is drawn into the cylinders. I have also seen carbon monoxide produced inside a cylinder of deco gas thanks to improper filling. Adiabatic compression had helped to vaporize the tank valve's high-pressure seat. Among the resulting cocktail of toxic gases – all of which had the potential to harm if breathed at depth – was carbon monoxide.

People suffering mild acute poisoning may complain of light-headedness, confusion, headaches, vertigo, and flu-like symptoms. Severe toxicity results in death. Going to any depth, but especially technical depths, with even a trace of carbon monoxide in one's breathing gas will result in severe toxicity.

This type of contamination is a threat anywhere in the world since carbon monoxide is colorless and odorless and difficult to detect without a sensor. Although rare, carbon monoxide poisoning is so serious that many divers carry and use portable CO-Sensors with them when travelling away from trusted fill stations. And a growing number of domestic compressor systems are now fitted with monitoring devices such as the AirSave System from IDE Compressors of Germany.

In a case before the California courts now, the family of a Canadian woman killed in Mexico by CO poisoning, have filed suit against PADI for what they allege is inadequate warnings about this type of threat in its student materials. Perhaps in the future, we will hear much more about the risks from this toxin and see CO sensors at dive sites more frequently than at present.

A MANAGEMENT STRATEGY

So, after all that preamble, each of us should have a good, clear understanding of why gas toxicity is a concern. Now we need to develop or adopt a strategy to make sure we limit the chances of gas toxicity being a dive buddy on our planned dives.

Actually, excellent guidelines already exist and are amazingly simple.

Let's start with Narcosis.

There are several equations we can use to calculate the narcotic loading of a gas on a particular dive, the narcotic loading of a specific gas, and the best gas to use for a controlled narcotic loading to a specific depth. I never bother with them. There is an easier way that needs zero understanding of how to solve an equation. I believe less algebra is better than a jam doughnut. So here is the simpler method originally shown to me by cave explorer Larry Green. I forget what he called it: probably something like the lazy-man method. I call it the Vacant Partial Pressure Method, but it is exactly what Larry showed me in 1994 and stolen blatantly from him.

Anyone who has taken and remembers a basic nitrox course will be familiar with the concepts of Acceptable Oxygen Partial Pressure. In a nut-shell, if we plan a dive with an acceptable oxygen partial pressure of 1.3 bar for our dive's maximum depth, we can easily work out what the best mix is for a specific depth. With a couple of additional key strokes on our pocket calculator (or smart phone), we can also work out the oxygen dose of specific gas at any depth, or the maximum operating depth (MOD) of a specific gas.

Often, basic nitrox students leave their class with the idea that a partial pressure of 1.4 bar of oxygen is the maximum acceptable level of oxygen for their dives. That's a slight over-simplification but it works for most if not ALL single recreational dives.

In the world of simple maths, we can refer to that 1.4 bar of oxygen as the acceptable oxygen depth. The actual depth in the water column can vary depending on the gas mix – 6 metres for pure O2, 21 metres for 50 percent, etc. – but the oxygen depth is constant.

We can and should do a similar exercise for Nitrogen! If we do, we can use the Vacant Partial Pressure Method to help manage gas toxicity: and that's our present goal. However, how many bar is a maximum acceptable level of nitrogen for our dives?

There isn't a hard answer to that as far as I can tell. Read the part on inert gas narcosis a few pages back and you'll understand why not. More importantly, I am reluctant to tell you that X-point-Y bar will work, because although your mate might be happy with that narcotic load, you may not.

COLD AND DARK EQUALS MORE NARCOSIS

But I can explain to you what works for a large number of folks, including me, when diving in cold (bottom of the Great Lakes cold) water.

At some point, a dive guru somewhere figured out that diving air to 30 metres / 100 feet delivers an "acceptable" narcotic load.

We can interpret this is several ways, but the most popular is to figure that the nitrogen load at 30 metres is acceptable. Therefore, since nitrogen partial pressure at 30 metres or 100 feet is 3.16 bar (ambient pressure x gas percentage = 4 bar x 0.79 = 3.16 bar). An acceptable nitrogen depth is 3.16 bar.

Next step, we add the oxygen depth to the nitrogen depth (1.4 + 3.16) and arrive at 4.46 bar. This then represents the acceptable total pressure, ambient pressure, depth (all three are the same thing). The is an acceptable depth for us to dive according to our simple maths Vacant Partial Pressure guidelines. Any deeper and we have a vacant partial pressure gap to fill with some other gas.

The metric unit divers have already worked out that 4.46 bar is the ambient pressure a 34.6 metres. The Americans in the audience need a calculator to arrive at 114 feet: because the ambient pressure at 114 feet is also 4.46 bar.

Ergo, if we plan to dive deeper than 34.6 metres or 114 feet we have a choice, break the "acceptable partial pressure" rule or fill the gap – any vacant partial pressure – with something else.

Here's how simple the calculations become. Say we wanted to dive to 45 metres / 150 feet. The ambient pressure down there is 5.5 bar. Step one, how much vacant partial pressure would there be. Pretty simple to work out: Subtract 4.46 bar (our combined oxygen and nitrogen depths) from the 5.5 ambient pressure / depth at 45 metres or 150 feet. The result: 5.5 – 4.46 = 1.04 bar.

This means that we have to add another gas – and helium is the only workable solution – to fill that gap.

Since the outcome of running down to our local dive shop and asking for a gas mix capable of delivering 1.4 bar of oxygen, 1.04 bar of helium, and 3.16 bar of nitrogen is likely to be hit and miss, we have one step left. We need to turn vulgar or common fractions into percentages, which are an altogether different species of fraction, and which is a process that's simpler than it sounds.

To do this for our example and all future calculations, the numerator (the integer above the line) will be the partial pressure of the gas whose percentage we want to find, and the denominator (the integer below the line) represents the ambient pressure. In our example above, the conversion to find the percentage of oxygen will be 1.4/5.5 = 25. Thus, the oxygen percentage we're looking to get in our mix is 25 percent.

Now for the helium, which is 1.04/5.5 = 19 percent (or close to it). The remainder will be nitrogen. (Convention is that we typically do not bother to write the nitrogen percentage on a request for mixed gas.)

In the real world, I believe most mix divers faced with these results would actually ask for a 25/20. If the dive were to be one of many in a series of multi-day exposures, the percentage of oxygen would likely be dropped a couple of points to help allay 24-hour CNS levels, and the helium might be bumped up for cold, working dives.

Whatever the final decisions on one's mix might be, vacant partial pressure calculations are simple and fast. The combined oxygen and nitrogen pressures remain constant and the remainder has to be helium: no equations to solve. Yippee!

Now oxygen toxicity.

The guidelines to manage potential hyperoxia are even more straightforward: Always analyse your gas; always label your cylinders. Due to a couple of recent accidents where the wrong gas was used and the wrong depth – with catastrophic results – it seems this advice is not clear enough. Let's expand on it a little in the hope of making it even more simple to grasp.

Analysers must be correctly calibrated and fuel cells (oxygen sensors) replaced according to their manufacture's recommendations, which is usually annually, sometimes sooner. If a cell does not line up with the results one expects from a known gas (compressed air is a favorite), then replace it with one that does.

Temperature and moisture influence the readings given by a cell, therefore it really helps stabilize and standardize results when the known gas – the gas with which cells are calibrated – has gone through a compressor filter system to remove moisture, and is at "room" temperature (about 20 C or 68 F).

Some folks wave an analyser around in the air to calibrate. This may be the only option open to us when there is no known calibration gas, and it's acceptable only if some adjustment can be made to account for temperature and humidity. (See chart below.)

In the many books on diving with nitrox, there are various suggestions and guidelines for labelling cylinders once analyzed. Pick the method that works for you, but again, I've learned a couple of tricks that may have kept me from making mistakes on dives.

I typically use a three-step system to label cylinders. All three steps make extensive use of duct tape. The picture above shows tape from the process of partial-pressure filling a stage with trimix, analysing it and marking it for diving. The tape at the top shows the gases to be added to the empty cylinder. Helium first to a pressure of 101 bar, then oxygen to 120 bar and finally top-up with air to the working pressure of 220 bar. (N.B. The half-filled in oblong for helium and empty one for oxygen and air, tells me that the filling process is only partially complete).

COMPENSATION CHART FOR CALIBRATING OXYGEN SENSORS IN ATMOSPHERIC AIR TAKING INTO ACCOUNT THE PRESENCE OF WATER VAPOR (HUMIDITY)

Relative Humidity	Air Temperature Degrees Celsius / Degrees Fahrenheit								
	0/32	4/10	10/50	16/60	21/70	27/80	32/90	38/100	43/110
10	20.9	20.9	20.9	20.9	20.8	20.8	20.8	20.8	20.7
20	20.9	20.9	20.8	20.8	20.8	20.8	20.7	20.6	20.5
30	20.9	20.8	20.8	20.8	20.7	20.7	20.6	20.5	20.4
40	20.8	20.8	20.8	20.7	20.7	20.6	20.5	20.4	20.2
50	20.8	20.8	20.8	20.7	20.6	20.5	20.4	20.2	20.0
60	20.8	20.8	20.7	20.7	20.6	20.5	20.3	20.1	19.8
70	20.8	20.8	20.7	20.6	20.5	20.4	20.2	19.9	19.6
80	20.8	20.8	20.7	20.6	20.5	20.3	20.1	19.8	19.5
90	20.8	20.7	20.7	20.6	20.4	20.3	20.0	19.7	19.3
100	20.8	20.7	20.6	20.5	20.4	20.2	19.9	19.5	19.1

When the Relative Humidity and Temperature meet in the black area of the chart, calibrate to the chart of use dry air to calibrate to maintain 0.5 percent accuracy with oxygen content.

Based on original data supplied by ANALOX Limited, Stokesley, North Yorkshire.

The tape in the middle shows the readings when the tank is filled, cooled and tested with an oxygen/helium analyser. The final readings are 18.1 percent oxygen and 43.6 percent helium, which is acceptable to me.

Step one is for mixing; Step two sees the mixing label replaced with an analysis label which shows gas percentages, date and final fill pressure; Step three tape replaces percentages and shows MOD in large numbers with the percentages of component gases much smaller.

The piece of tape on the bottom is one of two pieces that would be stuck either side of the cylinder's neck showing the MOD (maximum operating depth) of the mix. This last label has to be clearly visible, unambiguous and placed on opposite sides of the cylinder's neck, so that both you and your buddy can read them when confirming that it's OK to switch gas. (You will find a step-by-step procedure for gas switching in the chapter on operations.)

Labeling is as important when a gas mix is hypoxic, since breathing it on the surface can result in unconsciousness (and even death), and breathing it at the "wrong" depth in water can result in decompression complications or unconsciousness.

I follow similar procedure with mixing, analysis, and diving labels outlined above, but also mark the Minimum Operating Depth (above which the mix will deliver less than 0.18 ppO2) on the cylinder. Some divers also use the added precaution of placing tape with 'do not breathe' written on it over the valve.

In summary, know your limits for narcosis and stay within them, analyze, label, and double check breathing gases before getting into the water for odd tastes or smells, use monitors and sensors for other toxins such as carbon monoxide, buy gas fills from reputable suppliers who pay attention to their compressor systems and have their output tested by a known third party. Always and without exception, know what you are breathing... your life depends on that knowledge.

Chapter Six

EXPOSURE: How long; How deep; How cozy?

The Royal Mail Ship, Empress of Ireland, was an ocean-going luxury liner on her way to Liverpool from Quebec City when she sank in the Saint Lawrence River, 14 minutes after colliding with a Norwegian collier in the early morning fog of May 29, 1914. She had 1,477 people on board – passengers and crew – and the accident claimed the lives of 1,012: more than 800 of them passengers.

I've had the privilege to dive on this wreck several times; the first was in the aftermath of Hurricane Hortense, which blew its way up the eastern seaboard of North America, and although it did not hit Rimouski directly, turned that late Quebec summer into a mini maelstrom. The weather was awful: windy, wet and bleak. It had kept us out of the water and holed up in a small hotel for days playing euchre and praying for a break in the weather. When a narrow window of opportunity finally opened up early in the morning on our last scheduled day in French Canada, we suited up on at the dock, threw our gear onto our charter boat, and hoped for the best.

The dive was fantastic; truly historic, but my most vivid memory is staring at my dive computer towards to end of it and seeing that I had earned 45-minutes of decompression. The water was between three and five degrees Celsius (about 38 – 40 Fahrenheit). I had on inadequate thermal underwear, the current changed direction every few minutes and carried a force that varied from the relative comfort of a flag-waving three-quarters of a knot to an extremely unfriendly "hold your hat on Maude, we're going for a ride," three knots. The only up-side was a seal that seemed to delight in smart-bombing us relentlessly and at regular intervals throughout the various stops from about 9 metres to the surface. It took a liking to my fins.

I learned two lessons about "exposure" that day: never rely solely on a personal dive computer to track your decompression obligation (especially a second-generation dinosaur) because there might be a better way; and the speed at which time passes follows a curve proportional to falling water temperature.

Exposure in the context of diving and more especially risk management in diving, relates to surfacing safely without suffering decompression stress, hypothermia, heat-stroke, or wounding from passing critters; and without drifting off into the cosmos far from your comfortable ride back to harbor.

When dealing with exposure, the focus in most texts is primarily on the part of a dive that begins around the time we leave the bottom and ends when we are back on the surface (or more correctly, when our surface interval is over and we know we are safe from DCS). This is the usual emphasis since DCS is a real risk on all dives, even those on which broader issues such as staying warm and comfortable, surviving other environmental conditions such as current, boat traffic, wildlife; and even being able to pee when the need arises are always less compelling!

So, to conform to convention, let's start with that pesky decompression thing.

Following that first dive on the Empress, I understood viscerally that to follow a dive computer blindly and without question was not the best possible option. It can get one in over one's head, figuratively and literally. The PDC (personal dive computer) I was using – a demo from a European manufacturer – suggested I stay in freezing water and horrible conditions for far longer than necessary. Thankfully, my buddy and I carried lots and lots of "spare" decompression gas: most of which was consumed by the time our computers cleared us to surface, since both our respiration rates were easily double our norm.

Bear in mind, this episode was back in the dawn of personal dive computers. They were a reasonably new innovation, and those that did not lock-up when their user exceeded the no decompression limit (NDL), had strangely and well-padded degrees of conservatism built-in. What made the issue worse was that the user had zero jurisdiction over which level of conservatism was used.

It seemed that each manufacturer had its programmers conditioned to think like litigation lawyers. If the Bühlmann algorithm (and they all seemed to use Bühlmann back then... it was free after all) called for four minutes at six metres followed by 12 minutes at three, it would add time and stops automatically. In this case, something along the lines of a three-minute stop at nine metres and it would then increase the duration of "real stops" by 80 percent or more. So effectively, on a dive that would merit a stodgy, 16-minutes of deco time on tables, would have an ascent time twice as long using a PDC.

Modern PDCs are much more user-friendly even allowing divers to adjust levels of conservatism to suit their particular needs and proclivities. I wear one – occasionally two – especially for cave diving and when using a closed-circuit rebreather (CCR); however, I never dive without consulting custom dive tables created by using proprietary decompression software. This ensures me and my dive buddies are perfectly aware of the penalty we'll have to pay for hanging about as long and as deep as called for in the dive plan. It's simply part of our understanding of Exposure and its control.

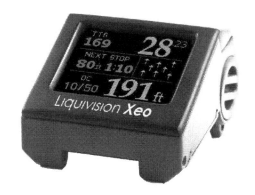

I want to explain something called ascent behavior. It's an emergency technique that came about because of the way I felt after that Empress dive, but before we go down that pathway, it's worth spending a few minutes explaining what works for me when it comes time to plan my personal decompression dives.

When I wear a PDC – usually when diving caves or multi-level wreck dives, it's always a fourth generation model such a this Liquivision Xeo. Compact, visible, reliable, and it backs up tables cut for the dive.

I use V-Planner. It is a software program originally created for PCs running Windows but which now runs on smart phones and tablets such as the Apple iPad.

When V-Planner was first launched by a guy called Ross Hemingway in the summer of 2001, there were other versions of custom decompression software on the market, and they worked fine, but the switch from those to V-Planner was almost epidemic... at least in technical diving circles.

V-Planner is based on the original research of Yount and Hoffman at the University of Hawaii. Their mathematical model uses bubble mechanics and dual-phase gas behavior to model what happens in a diver's body. For many technical divers, this seemed to be a better way than the old Haldanian tenets to model what actually happens to their body during a dive. I certainly felt more comfortable using decompression software based on this research than something known to be based on a faulty premise, which all Neo-Haldanian programs were. In short, bubbles do form in a diver's body during decompression, so best to adopt an decompression algorithm and ascent behavior that accounts for them.

VPM was further developed by Yount, Eric Maiken, and Erik Baker, and following diver feedback on earlier versions of V-Planner, Baker did more modifications and produced the VPM-B algorithm in 2002. Since then, V-Planner software has used the VPM-B algorithm. VPM stands for Varying Permeability Model. The B suffix simply indicates a more conservative interpolation.

The Coles Notes version is that VPM describes the change in state of the surface tension of the tiny bubbles of gas that are thought to form inside a diver as he or she ascends. If you read on, you will be introduced to my dump-truck analogy, and I am loath to spoil things by getting all scientific and geek-like here, so let's just say that VPM-B has become the most widely used bubble model decompression software among technical divers. It seems to work for a lot of people and has produced tables for some stellar exploratory dives.

Your experience may vary but I've used tables from V-Planner to guide me through more than 1,200 trimix dives, and countless decompression dives breathing nitrox without incident.

Using the software is very simple and the interface is extremely easy to learn and very user-friendly. The most important first step is to configure it in a way that suits your needs, including the conservatism factor. I do not intend to offer a blow-by-blow user-guide here, but for illustration only, here's a quick overview of what I usually do when using it to cut tables for open-circuit dives.

I set the conservatism in the mid-range. I believe the Nominal setting (zero conservatism) is the pure algorithm with each ascending "margin of safety" (from 1-5) making adjustments to the calculated critical bubble radius.

In other words, the more conservative it's set, the smaller sized bubble the program will allow to form in the diver's body (all hypothetical of course) during the ascent up the water column to the next stage of his or her decompression.

There are close to 40 user-adjustable settings. For example: oxygen narcotic or not; the oxygen depth of gas switches; extended stops after switches; depth of last stop; and overall descent and ascent rates.

A good exercise (and V-Planner is one of the best teaching tools for students of decompression because of this flexibility) is to set up a sample dive and play with settings to see what differences some of these user-controlled variables make.

As an example, the total run-time (head disappearing underwater until it pops back to the surface) for a simple 50-minute dive to 30 metres / 100 feet breathing an EAN32 (a typical tourist cave dive in North Florida), with the conservatism set to Nominal, is 65 minutes.

The program calls for a three-minute and 20-second stop at six-metres / 20 feet, followed by nine-minutes at three metres / 10 feet. If we simply crank the conservatism to level 5 (the most conservative), the same dive with exactly the same gas warrants an 84 minute runtime with a five-minute stop at nine metres / 30 feet; nine minutes at six metres / 20 feet; and 18 minutes at three metres / 10 feet.

Since the bottom time for both dives is the same 50 minutes, the 19 minutes difference in their runtime is ALL additional ascent time: 15 minutes of ascent time for Nominal conservatism compared to 34 minutes at level 5. Which one is correct?

I have no idea, what will work for you. In fact, there is no hard answer to that question. Certainly the 84-minute runtime is the safer option if we consider its potential to protect us from decompression sickness – at least at first blush. When we consider the relative safety of two or more ascent schedules, we have to take into account several issues. In particular how things such as extra time and different gas mixes might increase the risks of CNS oxygen toxicity.

In this specific case there would be virtually no difference since the additional stop time is spent not on an oxygen-rich decompression gas, but rather on back gas. Since the majority of additional time is spent a depths where back gas delivers an oxygen partial pressure far below 1.0 bar.

If the decompression portion of this dive were conducted breathing pure oxygen (a common practice) there would be a greater CNS loading for a "more conservative" dive: one that held the diver for longer at shallow depths where pure oxygen would be used.

Another consideration when comparing two or more schedules is the volume of additional gas required for longer ascent times. A longer decompression schedule may seem the better option until one realises that it require divers to break gas volume management rules.

Also, from a personal comfort viewpoint, thermal stress needs to be considered and accounted for. How would extra minutes in the water feel to a diver with a leaking drysuit… or inadequately dressed with strong current and an inquisitive seal to contend with? (For the record, I suspect the PDC that I wore on the Empress would have taken more like 95 minutes to clear after this dive.)

Oddly, the level of conservatism has a greater effect on runtimes than variations in the constituent gases being breathed. Here's a classic example of "ideal-world-think" vs. what actually happens on dive trips.

The plan is a wreck dive for 25 minutes to 60 metres / about 200 feet. A standard gas for this dive uses an 18/45 trimix (18 percent oxygen and 45 percent helium), with an EAN50 and pure oxygen as decompression gases. The total runtime for this dive at level 3 conservatism would be around 77 minutes according to V-Planner.

In the field (on location), partial-pressure mixing can present challenges especially when gas supplies are limited. So let's assume that the gas chosen to do the dive is an 18/35 – ten percent less helium. There may or may not be a noticeable difference to narcotic loading at depth (worth a test sometime, perhaps) but most inexperienced trimix divers might expect to see a difference in the ascent profile. Not at all.

The profile kicked out by V-Planner for the same dive using 18/35 instead of 18/45 delivers a 77-minute runtime. This is not an error, it's simply the way the mathematics work. There is a slight variation in the shape of the ascent curve at the shallower stops, but really not enough to worry much.

Therefore, the net effect of taking ten percent of the helium out of the mix is negligible.

However, if I flip the level of conservatism from +3 to Nominal and then back to +5 the runtimes vary considerably. Nominal conservatism, 18/45, nets a 68-minute runtime for the same 25-minute bottom time! At +5, same profile, same gases, the runtime becomes 86 minutes. (By the way, same kind of story using 18/35. Sixty seven minutes and 84 minutes respectively).

Playing this type of "what if" game with decompression software has taught me a couple of lessons that I feel are valuable.

Perhaps the most important is that getting all twisted and upset when my local fill station hands my sidemount cylinders back to me with an 18.4/42.9 trimix when I asked for an 18/45 is simply no big deal. I can not only use it and probably not know the difference at depth, more critically, I do not have to cut and learn new tables: The ones I already have in my head and backed up in my wetNotes will do just fine... and I know they work because I've "wet-tested" them several dozen times.

By the way, the same is essentially true with decompression gas. While on location a while back, our team ran out of oxygen and had to top off EAN 50 cylinders with compressed air. When analysed we each had something close to an EAN40. Apart from being able to switch from back gas to decompression gas earlier during our ascent at 30 metres / 100 feet, our ascent times were identical to those we had been running all week using EAN50 and switching at 21 metres / 70 feet.

This is NOT presented here to condone sloppy practices or lax controls but simply to point out that in the grand scheme of things, it's important to focus on what matters, and a couple of points here and there with one's breathing gases can be immaterial when it comes to decompression times even though they will alter MOD!

Perhaps this illustrates that decompression schedules are inherently sloppy and not something a scientist or engineer would put their signature to. From a control point of view, deco schedules are horribly ill-defined.

You could be forgiven for thinking that a huge difference in gas contents would make as much difference as cranking up or down a virtual control knob that influence the size of a hypothetical bubble. But it does not. What I find a sobering thought is that decompression calculations can deliver so many different outcomes and each of them is as "correct" as the other.

Perhaps the key "take-home" messages from that little self-congratulatory pat on my back above is that my primary dive tables are in my head. That may be a function of the fact that a 60-metre dive using the gases mentioned is not something I've done several dozen times, but possible closer to three or four hundred times. It may also be that I have taught myself deco-on-the-fly and ascent behavior. Knowing these two techniques makes the task of remembering deco schedules very, very simple.

After the Empress dive, when the feeling of cold left my body and I got sensation back in my extremities – probably a couple of months later – I started to think about what an ascent schedule (a decompression plan) actually was, and what it represented.

Until then, I'd never truly given profound thought to why or how a decompression algorithm worked. A strange admission since I was a trimix diver and teaching decompression diving. I'd read the books and listened to the lectures, and even had a couple of conversations with decompression theory 'experts' such as Bill Hamilton and John Cray, but I still thought that decompression was more science than the alchemy and black arts it actually is. I had much to learn.

In the past several years, the concepts and practices that frame decompression diving have evolved. Old-school Neo-Haldanian constructs have given way to Dual-Phase

Models, and the recreational dive community at large regards staged decompression as an acceptable norm and not the anathema it was branded as at one time. There are ordinary folk doing dives now that once only research, scientific, commercial and military divers undertook, and the recreational dive community has virtually unlimited access to information that can help inform our actions and highlight best practices.

There are still divers who have been taught that if they 'follow their computer' they will not get bent, but a growing number of divers, even pure sport divers, understand that DCS is a total crap shoot and there can be no guarantees: $1400 personal dive computers or not.

It would stretch credulity to tell you that decompression theory has been demystified for the average diver, but we have seen a rise in "alternate" deco options over the past decade or so. I wrote my first article on ascent behavior and deco-on-the-fly very soon after that Empress dive, and am now just one of a growing number of technical instructors who teach their students "alternate" deco strategies.

A couple of certification agencies include modules on Ratio Deco in their tech programs, and Mark Powell's excellent book *Deco for Divers* includes a segment on "making it up as you go along."

There is nothing magical about seat-of-the-pants decompression "tables." Deco-on-the-Fly is a contingency option when something goes pear-shaped, and not a PRIMARY scheduling tool. Deco-on-the-Fly is simply intended as a sense-check when cutting tables with decompression software such as V-Planner, as a backup if tables/computer is lost or malfunctions, or as a dive-planning tool.

It's also important to understand that although tables may vary, and extrapolation based on some "make it up as you go along" etiquette may all work to a point, for one's past experience with decompression schedules to have any value for future use, they have to be followed with some considerable accuracy. In a way, when we conduct a staged decompression dive, we are field testing a theory. That's why it is important to take notes – how we felt before, during and after the dive, the gases we used, the protocols we followed – and to follow the schedule we've opted to use: exactly.

There must be a baseline: a fixed non-variable. Perhaps more than one. Timing and buoyancy control are critical. If a schedule shows a three-minute stop at a specific depth, then stay for three minutes at that depth. Not a metre shallower and 30 seconds longer or shorter.

Speed is another non-variable. ALL algorithms, from the old US Navy tables through DCIEM's, PADI's, Bühlmann, VPM and so on, suggest a specific ascent speed. If a diver slows down or speeds up, they are essentially testing a new variant of the table, which may not be their intent: certainly if lack of control over ascent speed was a mistake. And when we roll the dice with decompression tables, sloppy control of ascent speed can be enough to buy us a trip to the chamber. Odd given the overall slop in the parameters but decompression is not fair or logical.

A practice that's grown in popularity among sport divers, but which is illogical as a strategy to avoid DCS, is adding "Deep Stops" arbitrarily. As I understand it a diver wearing a PDC and having no staged decompression obligation, stops for a minute or two during his ascent. In reality, this does nothing to minimize decompression stress and may actually add to bottom-time.

The better course of action, given that the diver is placing his trust in his PDC in the first place, is to follow the ascent speed it suggests rather than playing research diver.

Of course, as my episode on the Empress taught me, blindly following a dive computer is not the best option, but at least with a PDC strapped to his wrist, his ad-hoc violation of the ascent rate suggested by its algorithm will be noted and compensated for by the computer.

Perhaps more egregious are divers who do something similar when using pre-cut tables.

Their tables call for a brief stop at, let's say, 9 metres or 30 feet, so they believe by stopping for a couple of minutes at 18 metres / 60 feet or deeper, they are being more conservative. Not necessarily true at all; what they are doing is falling off the edge of the ascent schedule recommended by whatever decompression table they used to cut their tables. This practice is particularly ill advised when tables have been cut using a bubble model algorithm such as VPM.

I included a chapter in *The Six Skills* entitled **The Deco Curve: controlled ascent behavior and contingency decompression on the fly**. It covered the basics, and I don't think it makes much sense to reproduce the whole chapter here, but it's worth revisiting a couple of the central tenets to illustrate the "risk management" benefits of the practice.

The core of any "purple cow" usually includes a fresh look at an established concept: often, the whole cow is just a fresh look at an established concept.

Purple Cow is the title of a book by marketing guru Seth Godin. He tells us that to stand out in a market dominated by mega-corporations, so-so products, mass advertising and promotion, a new product or service (or idea) has to be remarkable and use basic word-of mouth, street-level promotional techniques.

He explains that when you drive by a herd of black and white cows every morning on your commute to the office, you'll stop noticing them. But if you drive by that same field and see a purple cow, you'll take notice and talk about it when you get to work.

Ratio Deco, Deco-on-the-Fly, seat of the pants deco, Ascent Behavior are all attempts at creating a purple cow. There is nothing earth-shatteringly new or blindingly brilliant about any of it.

The original work of Haldane, Workman, Lewis, Bühlmann, Yount et al, contains all the boiler-plates, nuts, bolts and other bits and pieces one needs to construct a purple cow. All you need is a creative way to think about decompression and decompression schedules.

A decompression algorithm describes a changing state over time. "State" is a theoretical construct that becomes a receptacle for compressed inert gas: for the record that theoretical construct is a diver. "Change" is the activity associated with the inert gas in the scenario (nitrogen and/or helium for the most part). In diving the activity being tracked is inert gas either going into the receptacle or coming out of the receptacle.

"Time" is also a factor as is depth. The compression phase of a dive is influenced by which gases are breathed on the bottom, the time spent underwater, and the depth. All these factors inform the decompression algorithm and it calculates how long it's going to take a diver to get from the bottom back to the surface without getting bent. Hold on. Let me rephrase that. The algorithm calculates the time it will take the diver to get back to the surface with a decent chance of not getting bent.

You and I have both read textbooks that claim the various tissue groups within a diver's body soak up, and release inert gases at different rates. These compression and decompression or on-gassing and off-gassing rates are the central strut of Haldanian decompression theory. There are N number of tissue groups each with a specific half-life – two minutes, four minutes, 720 minutes, whatever.

The textbooks tell us these tissue groups are designed to model the behavior of the human body. Based on modern research, common sense, empirical evidence, and scads and scads of data, it's clear they do not. They give us at best a sloppy, unscientific workaround. It suits our needs because it works: sometimes, but it is about as far from what happens as is possible while staying in the same zip code.

That's OK though: the only issue one might have with the tissue group half-life concept is that lots of people think tissue groups are actual science. They believe perhaps that a Sheldon Cooper-type with a stop-watch, white lab coat, access to an IBM zEnterprise EC12 mainframe, and a PhD in biomechanics has watched gas disappearing into and reappearing out of someone's bicep… or belly fat… in vivo with the aid of a magic microscope.

That would be nice, but it hasn't actually happened yet. Tissue groups relate to a diver's actual body parts about as much as Batman informs us about the night-time behavior of your average billionaire philanthropist.

Frankly, the picture does not come into much better focus with modern dual-phase theorems such as VPM or RGBM. As rock and roll legend Chuck Berry was fond of saying as he chicken-walked across the stage playing his big Gibson guitar: "Y'all know it's just a question of mathematics!" And that is all it is: a dash of calculus, some algebra, and a little salt and pepper.

The rest is made up, and has little to do with an actual living entity. Maths is a science but once someone tries to apply that science to a human being, all bets are off.

Once we accept that the application of mathematical solutions to a biological problem is hit and miss, it dawns on us that we are part of a huge experiment, foisted on us by PDCs and custom-cut tables.

Well, it may not actually be a conspiracy, but the hard and stark truth is that the only decompression schedules you can ascribe with any accuracy, and certainly the only ones you can be sure work for you, are the ones you have tested yourselves: and even those are iffy sometimes.

In essence, what all this amounts to is that the very best solution is to understand the best option available to preserve conservatism in one's decompression planning.

GAS TRANSPORT AND ASCENT BEHAVIOR

The biomechanics of inert gas transportation and storage is actually immaterial to our needs and not necessary to "understand" in order for us to "get" decompression theory. For example, we could agree that the diver's bloodstream is a network of roads and there are tiny dump-trucks using those roads to pick up and drop off loads of inert gas.

During on-gassing, these dump trucks arrive at the lungs (the distribution area), where they get loaded with inert gas by a large group of tiny members of the teamsters union. Loading completed – and this takes milliseconds – the dump trucks are driven to various warehouses around the body, where they dump their loads and head back to the lungs for a refill. The process is reversed during ascent. That's all we need to know.

There are a few vagaries, things that cause traffic to back up, police speed traps that cause slowdowns, the occasional accident that sees a truck tip over and lose its load (not a good outcome for anyone). From time-to-time, loading goes faster than expected and traffic is lighter so trucks travel faster. Sometime they take shortcuts. And as silly as all that may sound to a hyperbaric doctor, you and I actually need to understand no more about human physiology than that to make rational decisions about how long to spend at various points in the water column after exceeding a so-called NDL.

(Time to plagiarize my work from the *Six Skills*. The next few pages are lifted in part from Chapter Nine of that book. I've précised and edited, added some stuff, and hopefully made things easier to understand, but if you have read that book, you should recognize some of what follows.)

I want us to consider the suggestion that when we stand back and look at the collective outcomes of all the various algorithms and theories, tables and schedules we have to choose from, there is common ground among them.

In fact if we were to get a collection of decompression schedules for the same dive from a handful of different decompression models and compare them side-by-side, we might notice that each has a particular shape to it.

If we traced a graph tracking depth over time, the curve of each schedule would be slightly different but each would follow a similar shape; a variation on a flat parabolic curve.

What then if we were to learn the shape that curve makes: commit it to memory? Could that help us to understand decompression better? Would we be able to execute seemingly complex ascents from deep trimix dives more fluidly and with more fluency if we understood the mathematical mechanism that dictates the shape of that curve?

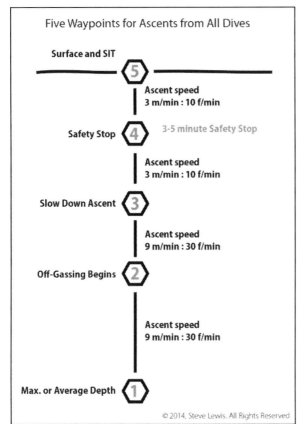

Five Waypoints for Ascents from All Dives

Surface and SIT

⑤

Ascent speed
3 m/min : 10 f/min

Safety Stop ④ 3-5 minute Safety Stop

Ascent speed
3 m/min : 10 f/min

Slow Down Ascent ③

Ascent speed
9 m/min : 30 f/min

Off-Gassing Begins ②

Ascent speed
9 m/min : 30 f/min

Max. or Average Depth ①

More to the point, would this greater understanding help us form the best possible contingency action if something should go wrong during a dive, and our original ascent plan had to be scrapped?

And that is the goal of the whole Deco-on-the-Fly exercise: an understanding deep enough to allow us to come up with a good alternative if our dive plan goes sideways for some reason.

Let's look first at something closer to home for an average diver than a deep trimix dive. We can use a simple example on the cusps between sport and technical: 40 metres (that's 132 feet) but within the NDL.

ONE BITE AT A TIME

First we need to appreciate that regardless of how complicated an ascent looks, the journey from a dive's maximum depth to the surface can be broken into bite-sized segments.

This goes for ALL recreational dives (sport and tech) whether they take place in 100 feet or 100 metres. The secret lays in first identifying five fundamental waypoints that **all** dives share:

1. Planned Maximum Depth or Actual Average Depth for multi-level dives
2. Off-Gassing Ceiling
3. First Running Stop
4. Staged Decompression Stop(s)
5. Surface and Surface Interval Time (an often neglected but important part of all dives including staged decompression dives)

The secret sauce is that a diver can behave in a sort of standard and fixed way when moving between these waypoints for ALL dives too. The only difference is in the final segment of a dive! Isn't that interesting?

It goes like this: the diver can ascend at nine metres or 30 feet per minute but no slower, between waypoints one and two.

This is the deepest part of the dive and below what's called the off-gassing ceiling (more about it later). Until a diver reaches waypoint two, he is still raking up bottom time. He is still on-gassing and adding to his inert gas load. Pickup trucks full of inert gases are actually moving both ways, but the traffic traveling from the body's gas warehouses to the lungs is starting to build; however, there are still more trucks dumping gas off than picking it up and carrying it back to the lungs to be exhaled.

This is no time to be moving slow. That comes later on near the surface.

Between waypoints two and three, the diver can move at nine metres or 30 feet per minute but no faster. The pickup truck traffic is now switching emphasis. More are picking up in the body and dumping at the lungs than the other way around. Decompression has begun. At this point a diver needs to be aware gas is leaving his body and it is critical that he has control over his ascent speed.

GET TO THE OFF-GASSING POINT AS SOON AS POSSIBLE

During the beginning of a diver's ascent – from EVERY dive – the travel between waypoints one and two can actually be at any speed. The 9 m/min. (30 f/min.) default is actually the minimum recommended speed. Any slower and the diver is essentially adding bottom time. Once the off-gassing ceiling is attained (waypoint two) and when travelling to waypoint three, ascent speed becomes critical.

Between waypoints three and four, the diver actually slows the ascent speed down to facilitate off-gassing and manage bubble formation. All phases of the ascent from any dive are critical – especially a dive that's deepish and longish like this one – but the part of the water column between waypoint 3 and 4 is super-critical even on sport dives.

The reason is that we are pretty sure bubbles do form in the body on even the most benign dive, and if they do, this is the theoretical danger zone where a speedy ascent will cause them to grow too fast for the dump trucks to handle comfortably.

Trying to carry one of these oversized bubbles can cause a truck to tip over spilling its load resulting in bubble trouble. Important to note that for a sport dive, stops are not necessary. All the diver has to do is slow his ascent to a meagre three metres or 10 feet per minute.

The technique of varying one's ascent speed is rarely taught to sport divers, and I have no idea why not. Perhaps someone in authority feels it presents too much of a challenge. (They used to say the same about nitrox.)

However, if you are a sport diver reading this book and you take nothing else from it, please consider learning this one trick. It seems that having sufficient control over one's ascent speed to slow down to a crawl when approaching the safety stop, conducting a safety stop, and continuing to the surface once again at a crawl, constitutes an excellent defense against "unearned DCS."

Let's continue our journey back to the surface. At waypoint four, the diver stops. For most recreational sport dives, a safety stop lasts for three to five minutes. It is optional, but recommended and certainly seems a great idea when surfacing from dives deeper than 25 metres / 80 feet or so.

Thus it has been included here. Safety stops are conducted at a depth somewhere between six metres and three metres (that's 20 and 10 feet).

When the safety stop is completed, the diver slowly floats to the surface no faster than three metres or ten feet per minute.
Yes, that really does translate into a couple of minutes to get from 6 metres (20 feet) to the surface!

One unknown entity in our waypoint example is the location of the off-gassing ceiling. For sport dives to 40 metres (132 feet), using nitrox or even air, we can peg it at around 30 percent of the way back to the surface. So for a 40-metre or 132-foot dive, the off-gassing will begin at a depth of 26.4 metres or 87 feet. For a dive to 30 metres, we can peg the off-gassing ceiling at around 19.8 metres. (So, for a 100-foot, the ceiling is around 66 feet.)

That is ascent behavior in a nutshell. If you were to run an example, you'd discover that a recreational dive to 40 metres/132 feet, about the limit for sport divers, would require between 13 and 14 minutes of ascent time.

This time includes a five-minute safety stop. Now if you're giggling silently to yourself and saying under your breath: "Silly tech divers, no sport diver is going to bother with such a slow ascent." I'd like to suggest you search the online internet forums for "unearned DCS hits."

To make this technique applicable to technical diving, we have to make a small adjustment.

Running stops (starting at waypoint three and also known by some folks as Deep Stops) are a series of brief stops that characterize ascent schedules typical of decompression profiles kicked out by dual-phase algorithms such as VPM. For our purposes, the first stop and the last stop in the series should each be two minutes. The remainder need to be one minute stops.

This effectively is the same as saying the diver moves between waypoints three and four at three metres per minute, with a one-minute stop at the first running stop and another one-minute stop at the last. Either way, the transit time between the two waypoints will add up to the same number of minutes.

The only other divergence is waypoint four – staged decompression stops rather than optional safety stops.

Everything up to this point is essentially the same regardless of the dive's profile. That is to say that every dive has a maximum or average depth, an off-gassing ceiling, running stops (or at least a portion of the ascent where the diver should slow down from nine metres a minute to three a minute), and a surface interval. But whereas sport dives have a single, simple safety stop, technical dives usually have at least one, and probably more, staged decompression stops intended to allow some time for the excess gas in the diver's body to be expelled during the normal breathing cycle.

Waypoint four is something that varies from dive-to-dive and person-to-person to some extent. On very deep and complex mixed-gas dives, waypoint four may start deeper than the depth limit for recreational sport diving, but even on a dive as extreme as that, the other waypoints are present!

APPLICATION
When I first published the first article about Deco-on-the-Fly, I had been teaching the technique to students for two years or so. It was not primarily intended to be a replacement for a set of tables cut by proprietary software such as V-Planner and then lost or misplaced (left back on the surface for example). Technical divers rarely lose tables, and if they do, another team member should have exactly the same schedule written down somewhere to share with them. Lost tables were not the actual problem.

What I saw as required was a cheap and cheerful way to create contingency tables on the fly if the actual bottom time for a dive differed from the times they'd cut tables for.

For instance, imagine that you and I are diving together and we have tables for 17, 20 and 25 minutes of bottom time at 45 metres (150 feet), but in some minor disaster, we got held up and stayed at depth for an extra four or five minutes: and so spent between 29 or 30 minutes on the bottom.

Our first step should be to get moving and to stop racking up bottom-time. This is when knowing ascent behavior comes to our aid. We know that for ALL dives, there is a point in the water column where the dump trucks travelling to our lungs to off-load excess gas begin to outnumber those moving in the other direction.

This is the off-gassing ceiling and the point at which decompression begins. Because something went pear-shaped and we overstay our allotted bottom-time, we need to get to this point as soon as possible.

It is critical to understand that moving off the bottom and heading shallower water immediately is more necessary than it is to know exactly how many minutes we need to stop at X metres or Y feet.

We can calculate the subtleties of the staged decompression phase of our dive later. Our immediate and primary consideration must be to get above the off-gassing ceiling. Once there we can begin to work out what comes next.

GET SHALLOWER BEFORE YOU HAVE TO THINK

Students of Deco-on-the-Fly, know that the off-gassing ceiling for this dive is going to be somewhere close to one-third of the distance to the surface: and one-third of 45 is 15. Therefore, we can immediately start heading up to a spot 15 metres closer to the surface. If we were using imperial units, one-third of 150 feet is 50 feet.

Another reason to get shallower is that at some point, we will have to do some calculations and make some key critical decisions.

Now at what depth do you think our mental capacity will be sharper: on the bottom or one-third of the way back to the surface? Regardless of what the narcotic load might have been at 45 metres / 150 feet, at 30 metres or 100 feet, it will be less… as will most other stressors.

Once we reach the off-gassing ceiling at around 30 metres or 100 feet, we have to make our first decision, and it's a reasonably minor one.

At the theoretical point where decompression begins and bubbles begin to form – in this case 30 metres or 100 feet – there are two schools of thought concerning what to do next.

The first school, let's call them the Micro-Bubblers, believe that a brief stop is called for – one or two minutes – a metre or so above the ceiling. This is NOT a deep stop or a running stop, those begin six to nine metres (20 – 30 feet) closer yet to the surface. This is simply a short pause to help manage bubble elimination.

The second school of thought is that once off-gassing begins, the best approach is to proceed to the next waypoint (waypoint 3) at a speed of 9 metres / 30 feet per minute to "drive bubble growth." This, for the record, is the default behavior written into V-Planner, so let's call it this school the V-Planners.

Now you and I have to decide which roll of the decompression dice we favor. Both offer us some benefits. Either way at this point, we know that by the time we reach waypoint 3 (which will be at around 23-21 metres / 75-70 feet) we are going to start our running stops.

In addition, at 21 metres / 72 feet, we will switch to our EAN50 decompression gas. Frankly, the decision whether we behave as Micro-Bubblers or V-Planners will have been made during our initial dive planning, so let's get moving.

In case you have not noticed, in our example you and I have travelled from the bottom, where we had an incident, to a point more than half-way to the surface without doing anything more that adjusting our ascent rate a little and executing a gas switch. No huge calculations, nothing to mess up. But now, at this point, we really do have to think, and do some simple arithmetic.

BARRE CHORDS: moving your decompression curve around in the water column

At this point, when I am teaching "Operations" to students, I ask if anyone plays guitar. I am constantly surprised how few guitarist take up scuba diving. It must have something to do with the fish... who knows.

So at this point, let's forget about diving for a moment and allow me to ask: "Do you play guitar?"

You can fib a little if you like. Even if your talents only extend to campfire songs or Guitar Hero. In fact, if at some point you've paid attention to any guitarist from Elvis Costello through Joey Strummer to Jonny Lang, you've seen someone play barre chords. When a guitarist slides her hand down the neck of her guitar and plays a chord, chances are better than not that she is playing a barre chord in some form or another.

The concept behind it is that if you move your fingers down the guitar neck you can to play totally different chords without changing the shape of your fingers.

For example, to play an A major chord (standard tuning, six-string guitar) one can strum all six strings while pressing down on the third, fourth and fifth strings at the second fret. (see the shape of the guitarist's fingers in the top frame on the left.)

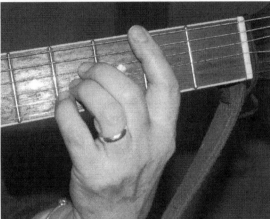

There are lots of other ways to get an A major chord out of a six string, but this is the default A Chord Shape.

If a guitar player moves that A shape down a couple of frets, keeping her fingers pressing down on the same three strings, while bridging the first, second and sixth strings with her index finger (exactly as shown in the lower frame of the picture), she is playing a B major barre chord.

Same shape and same intervals between the individual notes, but a different chord. Decompression schedules work in a similar way, and we can use that nugget of information to produce contingency schedules on the fly.

If we already know the "chord shape" for a specific dive (and if we have tables in our wetNotes as we should, we have a chord shape right in front of us), we can keep that shape but move the stops deeper in the water column for longer dives: and shallower for shorter ones. Just like a guitarist playing barre chords.

Let us consider a decompression schedule for a dive to 45 metres / 150 feet for 25 minutes.

This schedule was created using V-Planner and assumed 25/20 trimix for a bottom gas with EAN50 (MOD 21 metres / 72 feet) for the decompression.

The table provides a perfectly acceptable decompression plan. To use it for a diver that ran over time, we have simply moved the whole of our original down one stop deeper. Our two-minute stop at 12 metres / 40 feet is now done at 15 metres / 40 feet. The original nine-metres stop is now done at 12 and so on. Of course, there are some numbers missing. We have to fill in a value for the last stop at three metres or 10 feet. Easy. This is something we can do at leisure while conducting the deeper stops.

DEPTH m/ft	RUN TIME (STOP TIME)
45 / 150	25
21 / 70	28 (1)
18 / 60	29 (1)
15 / 50	30 (1)
12 / 40	32 (2)
9 / 30	35 (3)
6 / 20	40 (5)
3 / 10	49 (9)
SURFACE	50

Now here is the schedule adjusted for our five minute additional over-extended bottom time:

DEPTH m/ft	ORIGINAL SCHEDULE	CONTINGENCY SCHEDULE
45 / 150	25	30
21 / 70	28 (1)	33 (1)
18 / 60	29 (1)	34 (1)
15 / 50	30 (1)	36 (2)
12 / 40	32 (2)	39 (3)
9 / 30	35 (3)	44 (5)
6 / 20	40 (5)	53 (9)
3 / 10	49 (9)	?? (??)
SURFACE	50	60 (Because of the 1:1 ratio of bottom time to ascent time.)

Since we know the ratio of ascent time to bottom time for the depth and gases being used (in the case of our 45 metre / 150 foot dive that ratio is 1:1) we add a value for that last stop that brings our total ascent time into line with the desired total. In this case we need a total of 30 minutes ascent time. When we leave our 6-metre / 20-foot stop, we will have spent 23 minutes (surfacing: 30 minutes bottom time subtracted from a 53-minute runtime). This means the missing numbers should be a runtime of 60 minutes with a stop time of seven (7). Our arrival on the surface will be one minute later or a total runtime of 61 minutes.

If the situation had arisen where we were unsure of the ratio of bottom time to ascent time, it's reasonably easy to work out: we could have simply looked at the profile we created for the 25-minute dive! Chances are extraordinarily good that the ratio for 30 minutes will be the same. In other words, if a 25-minute bottom time generated about 25-minutes of ascent time, then a 30-minute bottom time will require about 30 minutes of ascent time. It really is that simple especially at depths of less than 7 bar (60 metres).

WAYPOINT FOUR: DECOMPRESSION STOPS

A final word about Deco-on-the-Fly. When we want to create an ascent schedule based on Deco-on-the-Fly principals there are a few simple 'guidelines' we must work within:

- Understand that there is a relationship between bottom time and required ascent time. This varies a bit with depth and gases used, but when you cut tables with deco software, commit this ratio to memory
- Remove as many variables as possible (standard ascent behavior, standard gases)
- This system works for dives between 42 metres and 75 metres
- The off-gassing ceiling is 1.5 bar (one and a half atmospheres, 15 metres or approximately 50 feet) shallower than the max depth
- Running stops can start immediately above or up to 10 metres above the off-gassing ceiling
- Running stops are one or two minutes long and the maximum number of running stops is five
- Gas switches must be made according to the MOD of the mix (e.g. the MOD of the standard EAN50 is 21 metres or 72 feet)
- Spend at least four minutes at the depth where gas switches are done. Follow the normal shape of the curve from that point on up
- A staged decompression stop's duration is a minimum of three minutes
- Decompression stops are part of a short series that conforms to a simple mathematical pattern that is unique for each gas
- Each series consists of blocks of five numbers that fits within the operational limits of a decompression gas and consists of five evenly spaced stops the total duration of which adds up to a specific ratio of the total bottom time
- A gas switch reset the series and the blocks of numbers repeat through the range of each decompression gas used during ascent
- A close fit works; do not fret details as long as the total time spent completing each series of stops adds up to the required value
- Take notes. Always track what works for you. Deco-on-the-Fly is a guideline and there is nothing sacrosanct about it. Where there is a degree of latitude, write down what worked and if you have to do it again, follow a similar approach.

In closing off this particular portion of Operations, let's review a few points that relate to decompression planning in general.

1. Decompression algorithms are just pure mathematics trying to model biology
2. Biology is weird and is difficult to model with pure mathematics
3. Decompression theories contain varying amounts of guesswork – some more than others since goats and Jello do not supply intellectual feedback
4. Given all the above, you realize and accept that by conducting staged decompression dives, you have become part of the experiment. TAKE LAB NOTES!
5. Decompression theory is constantly being refined (The only constant is change)
6. There is no such thing as a foolproof decompression schedule
7. Decompression is affected by several variables: some, like hydration, we can control, and others we cannot.
8. Whenever you exit the water after a staged decompression dive – and regardless of what your decompression schedule or (gods forbid) your computer is telling you, LISTEN to what your BODY is TELLING YOU.
9. Given a few basic rules and some simple "memory work" almost anyone can produce an *ad hoc* ascent schedule that will work... sometimes.

At this point, I need to remind you that any deviation from an established and tested decompression schedule is risky. This Deco on the Fly stuff is simply better, in my opinion, that not knowing what to do in the event of some sort of kit failure of other contingency. It has worked for me and many of my students, but it may not work for you at all. You may think it makes less sense than juggling Tom cats, and I respect that!

ROUGH WATER, STRONG CURRENTS & OTHER ISSUES

Seasickness is a fact of life for many, many divers. It's said that everyone gets sick, some more easily than others. I read somewhere that three out of every four astronauts get sick to some degree during their first few days in space. And a buddy who served for many years as an officer on a variety of naval vessels large and small assured me, as I moaned that the deck of the boat we were on was moving too much, that anyone who says they have never been seasick is either a fair-weather sailor or have not been to sea.

Anyway, if you are a sufferer, you have my sympathies. There is not much to be done from an operations point of view to alleviate your situation, but there are a couple of tips and some warnings to share.

As an open water diver, you were probably told that if you got nauseous underwater, keep the regulator in your mouth, hold it in when throwing up and have a backup ready. I have zero to offer in the way of advice informed by experience on this score. Most of the folks I know and dive with would, I believe, rather not test the concept. For my part, if I felt as though I were about to throw up, jumping in the water would be the last thing on my to-do list. I simply cannot imagine vomiting and having 20, 30, 40 minutes or more of decompression to complete.

Which of course brings us to the topic of medications. Simply put, over-the-counter remedies such as dimenhydrinate, meclizine, diphenhydramine, cyclizine, and scopolamine all have some side-effects – usually drowsiness – but there is too much variation from individual to individual for there to be a safe recommendation.

I believe that if you are going to take part in advanced diving, don't take any of them at all. Or if you absolutely must, get the advice of a physician. Preferably a doctor who dives and who understands the type of diving you engage in.

Alternative options include ginger. I use ginger and carry it with me on most dive trips. It works for some people and not for others. Ginger lovers use the root – very inexpensive but an acquired taste for sure – ginger candies and candied ginger, and ginger pills. Best I can suggest is to try it for yourself and I hope it works for you.

Some people have success wearing special bracelets – sea bands, bio-bands and the like. These may also work for you and in any event are inexpensive and certainly drug-free.

My naval buddy swore that the best cure – apart from time, as most people do get used to the motion of a boat after a day or two – was a *Dark and Stormy*: a 'nourishing mix' (his words) of black navy rum, ginger beer (nothing at all like ginger ale), and grenadine. I have tried it many times – but only after diving. It's a magnificent drink, but more study is needed.

Three things to avoid at breakfast when getting ready for a charter are: citrus, coffee and eggs: anything in fact that's acidic. My perfect "day on a boat" breakfast is plenty of water, oatmeal with a little brown sugar, and ripe mango. Try it, it might work for you too.

Spectacularly heavy seas – not the stuff of surfing movies but swells and waves around two metres or about six to eight feet – worry me, but not because of motion sickness. Getting off a pitching boat is child's play, but getting back on wearing full kit for a decompression dive can be a true adventure.

Since the primary concern is always safety, use good judgement to call a dive on weather and sea conditions. Plan for a blow-day in your trip itinerary, especially on small islands with lots of distance between them and a continent for waves to build. Take it easy, or perhaps get to the lee shore and paddle around there.

Falling to the deck of a pitching boat, while wearing steel doubles or a rebreather and stage bottles – even falling over on a pitching boat with nothing but a pair of shorts and a t-shirt on – can hurt: a lot. A fall can also have tragic consequences. A friend told me of a diver she knew who died after falling on his stage bottle. Unknowingly he ruptured his liver and suffered from a catastrophic bleed and died.

A 'NEW' MENACE: SIPE

Swimming induced pulmonary edema (SIPE) has been described as drowning on your own bodily fluids. Up until very recently, I knew of only one instance of SIPE in a recreational diver. During the past two to three years, I've read about more than a dozen.

SIPE, it seems is an emerging condition. For the most part it affects fit individuals, and in most of the incidents involving scuba divers, they have also been triathletes.

SIPE symptoms include acute respiratory distress, wet-sounding popping or crackling in the lungs, a gurgling cough, and pink frothy blood-tinged sputum. The issue with SIPE at depth is shortness of breath. For a diver this sensation can cause panic and result in a tragic outcome. The causes of SIPE are not fully understood, but we do know that whatever the trigger or triggers may be, the immediate problem is liquid from the capillary beds surrounding the victim's alveoli leaking into the lungs. The work of breathing then becomes progressively higher.

Since little is known about causes, is also not clear what predisposes one to its occurrence or recurrence, and even the currently cited correlation with triathletes (especially females) may be misleading. The best we can say is that SIPE is an issue to be aware of. If you experience any unexpected increase in the work of breathing during a dive, bailout without hesitation.

WARMTH & COMFORT

It would be remiss in a book concerned with risk management, in a chapter on operations, not to mention thermal protection – which in water at less than "bathtub" temperatures means a drysuit in my books – and the consequences of adequate hydration when diving in said drysuit.

Many divers who have been lucky enough to experience only water temps in the upper twenties through mid-thirties (think a few degrees north or south of the equator) don't understand drysuits. Some who dive in temperate zones, don't grasp the concept either, and there are folks who ice dive in wetsuits.

Even when I am breathing moist, warm gas from a rebreather, I feel the cold and always did. Age makes the issue more of an issue. On open-circuit too, the feeling is worse. Therefore, most of the diving I've done has been in a drysuit of some sort. I have logged dives in a wetsuit and conducted decompression dives and cave penetrations "wet," but rarely. For comfort before, during and post dive, I believe a drysuit is how to ensure personal comfort and keep hypothermia at bay.

Staying warm (and dry) is a safely concern because humans don't do cold very well. What is called Primary Hypothermia comes about after exposure to cold air or immersion in cold water. Cold air we have all experienced -- think Christmas shopping, light sweater, flat-tire, freeway.

Even in moderate air temperatures well above freezing, hypothermia is possible but may take several hours to develop. Immersion hypothermia can occur within minutes of entering the water since water draws heat away from the body much faster than air does.

Not only is feeling cold uncomfortable, even mild hypothermia will cause some degree of mental confusion (I believe any effect of inert-gas narcosis is greatly magnified by cold). Mild hypothermia will also negatively affect coordination and the ability to move efficiently. Serious hypothermia can result in irregular heartbeat, stupor, and the related complication of passing out while underwater.

By definition, decompression dives mean longer times at depth and longer times than getting back to the surface, and the consequences of cutting a decompression short because of being cold are serious enough to render the option not an option at all.

There are also complications to the process of off-gassing due to the human body's defense against mild hypothermia (basically shunting blood to the body's core and shutting peripheral blood flow to a trickle). Also a dive computer may display a temperature reading but it does not take it into account when calculating decompression obligations how a diver is dressed. The algorithm makes its calculations assuming the diver is warm, well-fed and well-rested. A cold diver is not part of the on-gassing/off-gassing balancing act it is performing.

Thermal protection is a function of being dry (a condition supplied by the suit), and being warm (which is a function of the undergarments worn under the suit creating "loft," wicking away perspiration, and trapping body heat through the use of various materials).

Worth noting as well: hypothermia also offers a real threat during surface intervals, during which times winds can accelerate evaporation from wet clothes (including drysuits) creating a huge problem for folks who want to make a repetitive dive; or who are on a boat or in an area with little shelter.

One of the spots in the world boasting truly exciting wrecks is the Great Lakes basin… the eastern edge of which is approximately a 12-hour drive west of the site of the Empress of Ireland, and its western shore another 17-hours further on. These are

Lakes Ontario, Erie, Huron, Michigan and Superior traveling from east to west. In summer, air temperatures can reach the low to mid-30s (that's around 90 F) with high humidity. However, the water at depth is a more or less constant 4 degrees (that's 38 F).

One has to dress warmly for the bottom, but hanging around on the surface dressed in a drysuit and thermal undies can cause hyperthermia: too much heat. This condition creates problems for divers too.

Each of us finds strategies to avoid both unwelcome states, but here are a couple of things that have helped me.

I have resisted the temptation to recommend too many particular brands of kit in the past six or seven chapters, but I simply have to put in a plug for O'Three Drysuits out of the U.K.

A PLUG FOR MY FAVORITE DRYSUIT

The thing about drysuits is they come in many flavors. The most common being vulcanized rubber, special fabrics with butyl rubber sandwiched between them (called trilaminate), various types of neoprene, even tacky plastic bag-like things with elastic coveralls to make them fit... well, to attempt a fit.

There are pros and cons with each and if you ask 20 divers for their opinions, it is unlikely that you will get the same list of likes and dislikes from more than two of them. However, I'd like to share a personal experience, based on 20-odd years of drysuit use... some more odd than others.

A couple of years ago, I was approached by a UK manufacturer of suit "systems," which is usually a fancy marketing term for suits, undies and accessories like hoods and bags and gloves. They asked me to try one of their suits. It was January, I was going to North Florida to help teach a CCR class in the caves there.

In January, the Florida panhandle can get cold (below freezing), at least on the surface. The water is a pretty constant 20 degrees Celsius (that's 68 in old money). I took the suit.

It was comfortable, warm, dry and quite a bit more streamlined swimming in the caves than I would have been dressed in the trilaminate suit I took as a backup. More remarkable perhaps was that my trilaminate suit was a custom cave-cut suit and the British one was off-the-rank.

Anyhow, to cut to the point, I now have two O'Three neoprene drysuits, the original Ri 2-100 that I took to the panhandle and a custom-cut Ri 1-100 that has become my go-to suit for most dives. Between them they have several hundred dry, comfortable, warm dives. They have kept the cold and wet out in caves, on wrecks, in warm water and freezing water. I have never had a better-made, better-designed, more durable suit.

The author's O'Three Ri 1-100 drysuit conforms to a long list of desirable features and benefits required of it. It is rugged, well-made, comfortable, dry and streamlined. It's also fully accessorized and guaranteed against defect by its UK manufacturers.

Your experience and needs may differ, but here are some of the things to look for in a drysuit.

It should fit particularly in the legs, shoulders and hips. I have seen divers fight suits that are too tight or too baggy. A lot of trilam suits, the ones with telescopic bodies particularly, seem to have lots of spare material. This creates drag in the water and if extreme, adds a level of complication to trim and buoyancy control.

Same overall issue with heavy neoprene suits that are so difficult to move in that divers lose the ability to move their arms and legs freely: which can cause problems unless you intend to lay on the seabed like a clam.

A drysuit should keep you dry. I have had very expensive U.S.-made suits that were as water-tight as my Aunty Fanny's lace hanky. Price and reputation notwithstanding, the secret is in the quality assurance process after suits come off the production line (and the manufacturing process itself after a fashion).

When shopping for a suit, don't be lulled into believing that XYZ brand is a good buy because it's expensive. There are several brands half-the price of the leading trilam suits that are a better investment, in my opinion. This is especially true if your diving is infrequent and you log less than 100 dives a year.

A suit must be rugged enough to hold up to the conditions where you dive. I took a brand-new trilam suit scooter diving on a small wreck off the New Jersey coast many years ago. A slight brush with the wreck (I remember it as such but it may have been more of a bump), and I had several litres (there are 3.8 litres to a US gallon) of seawater joining me inside my sparkly new suit.

It should also have the accessories you need to make your diving easier: pockets, gloves, out-board dump or pee-valve. All of these contribute to comfort and one might say that safety starts with comfort. Certainly being uncomfortable can cause us to take shortcuts.

The pee-valve is a case in point. In my opinion, doing long dives without one, and staying comfortable is close to impossible. It may be a function of age but I have spent final minutes on a decompression stop unable to focus on anything but the fact that I did not connect my pee valve and "I really need to go... now." I know people who have cut decompressions short in order to get out of the water and relieve themselves.

Fitting a drysuit with a pee-valve (or off-board dump in polite society) is actually a simple job but better left to the manufacturer to install when the suit is first ordered. I have used balanced and unbalanced, and both function just fine. My preference is to have a balanced valve since it needs no "priming" before the dive and one does not need to coordinate the act of peeing with opening the outboard end of the system – usually by turning a valve or loosening a bolt – and then closing it when finished. This is a skill not required when using a balanced valve.

Three pieces of Pee-Valve advice from someone who has learned his lessons the hard way.

1. Keep it clean. I disinfect the workings after every dive with a 10 percent solution of Dettol. The active ingredient in Dettol is a chloroxylenol but it smells of pine oil and is an effective disinfectant used in hospitals and by Moms with scruffy kids in the UK when I was growing up.
2. Prepare the area. Man or woman the method of connecting you to the plumbing differs somewhat. For men it's an external condom catheter and for a woman something that looks like a cross between an oxygen mask and an athletic cup. Regardless, there is adhesive involved. Safety razors (disposable for sensitive skin) are recommended. Post-dive, I have found baby wipes remarkably handy for cleaning up reside glue, since a build-up of sticky is not something you want to experience.
3. Male external condom catheters are available from several manufacturers and in different sizes. Size really does matter. Buy what fits, and if you have doubts, most drug stores / pharmacies specializing in these products can supply you with a size chart! When I can get them, I think Conveen® catheters are the best.

Lastly, let's looks at a drysuit accessory that is vitally important. For the most part, undergarments and not the suit are what keeps a drysuit diver warm and comfortable.

Again, these should fit, be comfortable, compact, easy to clean and modular. The bottom layer should have the ability to wick perspiration away from the diver, the outer layer should offer some protection from wind and weather when the diver is on the surface, and the whole garment should offer a degree of protection from the cold even if one's drysuit springs a leak.

I have undergarments from various manufacturers and in various weights which I mix and match as temperatures dictate. The premium brands in my experience are Santi, fourth element, and O'Three. Again, much like so many other things, fit is form and becomes function. Too loose and you will have trouble with buoyancy and trim; too tight and you will be unable to reach things you really want to reach when diving… like valves.

Chapter Seven

EQUIPMENT: DOING WHAT WORKS:
a slightly different philosophy

The single topic most open to debate and armchair quarterback syndrome among divers is dive gear. In particular it presents the broadest source of confusion and controversy for a huge percentage of those making the switch from sport diver to deep or technical diver. For most folks, the questions center on how much of it to buy, which brand or brand(s), from whom, and when they get it home, how to configure it.

The first question most who are midway through their transition from sport to tech ask is: "do I have to buy all new gear or will my old stuff do for a season or two?"

A close second is: "Should I go backplate and wing or sidemount?"

In between number two and what is usually the final plea for assistance – "I think I would like a rebreather, so what's the cheapest one that's any good?" – the list of questions is long and close to overwhelming. Among them, whether a drysuit is more dangerous than a wetsuit, which brand of regulators is to scuba what Gibson Guitars are to rock music, hints on how to do a reverse frog-kick using split fins – which some punter from the outskirts of Birmingham insists are the best swimming-aid since legs – and which kind of computer to buy for decompression diving.

When Sheck Exley drew up his original risk management guidelines, the intended primary hint was about how risky it is to do a dive with improper, inappropriate or too few dive lights. He did not mention the whole equipment package, and certainly did not promote a specific brand or kit configuration. Life was different then: simpler perhaps. The Pet Shop Boys' hit "West End Girls" was creeping up the Billboard Charts; "Blue Velvet," David Lynch's bizarre and compelling cult movie starring Kyle MacLachlan, Isabella Rossellini, Dennis Hopper and Laura Dern was playing at local art cinemas;

and the Ford Taurus was introduced into the North American car market. Kit choices for any diver – especially a cave diver – were limited, and less attention was paid to form than to function. Broadly speaking, if it looked like it might work, you strapped it on and went cave diving.

A few years later, when Exley's admonition to "carry at least three lights [when cave diving]" had evolved into the far more inclusive 'Equipment,' many other things had also changed. A Canadian baseball team won the World Series that year; Laura Dern was in another cult movie, but a more successful box office hit, called Jurassic Park; and UB40, yet another UK band, was topping the charts singing *I Can't Help Falling In Love*.

DIVE GEAR WAS SUDDENLY MORE OF A DISCUSSION POINT

In 1993, the warning about carrying the right equipment had to cover the backsides of a new and growing batch of technical divers making deep and long excursions into plenty of places that had no resemblance to a cave. Carrying enough lights was never going to make the difference between those divers getting back to the surface or not. Function was still more important than form, but the distance between them was narrowing. Kit choices had expanded, and a well-outfitted technical diver was starting to follow some standard guidelines. Her gear also looked much less like it had been cobbled together by a band of DIY elves.

Equipment continues to change more than 20 years later, and will carry on changing as long as advanced scuba diving grows more and more popular. Change, evolution, even revolution are the only constants in life and certainly change governs just about every aspect of the gear we use to explore underwater.

What was top-shelf and best practice just a few years ago, wouldn't even make the bloopers reel now. Take dive lights as an example. New technology, new manufacturing processes, and cut-throat competition mean that a diver can buy a $100 handheld light the size of a dill pickle that kicks out almost as many lumens as a canister light that cost more than $1000 five or six years ago.

What we do has changed too. Normal everyday events in diving now include regular people, not military personnel or scientists or commercial divers, just ordinary weekend warriors doing dives that require the first staged decompression stop to be deeper than the recreational sport diving limit of 40 metres or 130 feet. The window displays in local dive stores, which a couple of years ago were up in arms rallying against tech-diving, now feature stage bottles and scooters and all-black dive gear: the pink and yellow fins were hidden away in the store-room out back. Even run-of-the-mill, bog-standard sport-diving instructors, once in the vanguard of those against teaching nitrox because it was "too complicated and would get people killed," now offer technical diving programs sanctioned by the same agency that initially banned nitrox.

This growth and the commercial pull of advanced diving, has driven every manufacturer and their aunt Nelly to make gear for "technical diving." In some cases, form truly does follow function. The average deep trimix diver today has never had to cultivate a friendship with the owner of an industrial sewing machine. There is a store-bought version of just about everything one needs to dive just about anywhere. And that is a change for the better… mostly.

Equipment is still a pain in the rump. It's still heavy, and it seems to get more expensive. On the positive side though, once-up-a-time dive kit required its users to accept compromise. Often, one simply could not buy gear that was a perfect fit for the job one wanted it to do. One made it oneself or one compromised. That aspect of diving has passed for those who pay attention.

I am not a gear aficionado. I do not drool or faun over dive gear. I save that for well-made guitars, luxury wristwatches (a Ulysse Nardin marine chronometer please), vintage wooden boats, and beautiful sports cars.

To me all gear is evil, a necessary evil, but evil nevertheless. I have developed a sort of bipolar love-hate posture towards it. I do concede, however, that the breadth of choice is mostly a good thing.

There are many books and websites dedicated solely on equipment configuration: how to tie a bolt snap to a backup light and which shoulder to strap it to.

In previous books and articles, I've thrown my hat into the "Hogarthian" ring and there is a quick summary of my interpretation of its rules and guidelines at the end of this chapter for those of you interested in what informs the Doing What Works approach I use and teach.

Overall though, especially in a book about risk management, how one configures one's dive gear, is a small component of the whole. And that whole includes how to select it, how to look after it and how one configures one's mind to react when a piece of kit goes wrong… and it WILL go wrong. In other words, from a risk management perspective, form, function and fit-for-purpose are so closely aligned that it's almost impossible to slide a credit card between them.

And just in case you fall into the category of reader who is just beginning their journey into advanced diving, a credit card will be useful besides trying to slip it between seemingly abstract concepts.

Most of us, when it comes to buying new dive gear – and if you are new to advanced diving, most of your previous kit will be unsuitable and you will be buying new gear – most of us are looking for a quick tip to govern our buying habits over the next few months. The best I can do is this.

PACK LIGHT AND LEAVE THE CLUTTER BEHIND

I have found that advanced diving has more in common with extreme mountain climbing than most other sports; and certainly has a few things to learn from it. Ernest Hemmingway judged auto racing, bull fighting, and mountain climbing as the only real sports (he said all the rest were games), and although I'd love to know what he'd make of technical diving, my allusions have less to do with machismo and more to do with the things both climbers and divers go through to get mentally and physically prepped to do their thing.

There is also one other thing. Mountain climbers, the ones that make it back down safely, seem to have a knack for knowing what gear to take and what to leave behind. This too is a valuable skill for a diver.

If there's one trigger that plays a major role in more mishaps and near-misses than any other, it has to be task-loading. Trying to carry too much crap. Simple solution, if you don't need it, don't take it. Schlepping more equipment than you need carries an unacceptable level of risk, so one should resist the temptation to do it.

That said, we might concentrate on a couple of specific bits of kit that would be considered extra or even superfluous by many sport divers but that in fact provide an essential function: a stage or deco bottle with regulator; and a DSMB with spool. If you are making the transition to tech from sport diving, these are purchases that will most definitely be in your future. Using these as examples may also highlight some of the basic tenets behind the DW^2 philosophy.

I cannot give any unique tips on what's called: Traditional North Florida Cave Gear – backplate, wing, long-hose, and stage bottles hanging like ornaments on a Christmas tree at the Mad Hatter's Tea Party. I dived a backplate, wing and doubles for many years but no longer do so. Not because there is anything wrong with the system. There is not, it works fine and is the right configuration for many situations. If done correctly, it is also a great configuration from an accident prevention and risk management perspective.

From what one sees at dive sites and reads in various onLine forums, this kit has not evolved much since a bunch of cave divers came up with the basic concept of using a backplate and breathing the longhose back in the 1980s. The argument whether to wear the cord from one's canister light over or under the long-hose, prattles on seemingly without an end in sight, but the basics remain the same. Because it's a well-established configuration, there are plenty of resources to draw information from, and really not much need to rehash anything about it here.

The easiest way to find trim and control buoyancy in this configuration is to wear tanks that fit and a wing matched to those tanks. The standard advice to breathe a longhose connected to the right-hand tank, wear a bungeed backup around one's neck, have a simple SPG on one's left hip, and a simple webbing harness, all hold good.

When I dive open-circuit from choice – which is surprisingly often for a "rebreather diver" – I dive a sidemount configuration (SM), and it is that configuration I feel most comfortable offering suggestions about. Sidemount is not perfect since nothing can claim to be. It is the most versatile configuration generally speaking, and it can work well for OC diving whether in open water or an overhead environment.

My very first experience on scuba was as a kid dry-caving in the UK. Looking back at that experience, I shudder and also realise we side-mounted our kit. It would make me feel like a SM guru if I were able to tell you that those early adventures in England's Mendip Hills had a strong influence over my dive habits now. But that would be total hogwash. What I dive, promote and teach now is about as different to what was in use then as an Audi R8 Spyder convertible is to a Model T Ford. Apart from the shared fact that apparatus then and now both get wet, absolutely nothing else seems related or relevant.

This is one reason I am reluctant to get too deeply into specific brands and models. Who knows, next year I may be contrasting Model T Fords against a 500 horse-power electric car... or a jetpack!

However, we do have to be specific enough to make our point, and so now is when I have to declare a conflict of interest.

As a consultant in the dive industry, I work with equipment companies: manufactures and distributors. For the most part, the products I work with are the brands I recommend. I do not get an endorsement fee to mention them here or in a classroom/course setting. I do it because I like the way these brands tackle design, component selection, production, quality assurance, and customer service.

I hope my opinions are objective, I try to keep them that way, but there is a potential for an outside observer to think otherwise, and I wanted to be upfront. In the final analysis, with very few exceptions, the difference between a make and model of something mentioned here and Brand X might be quite superficial in any case.

My reason for choosing one above the other may be something as relatively minor as the way it is possible to route low-pressure hoses coming off a first stage, or the angle of the beam of light produced by a backup light. In the overall scheme of things, these are trivial issues… certainly compared to real challenges such as simplicity, suitability and reliability.

To muddy the waters even more, you will find plenty of fellow divers who will swear by all that's holy that the particular gear configuration or brand of kit that they use is the best thing since the Chillicothe Baking Company, began to sell loaves of **Kleen Maid** Sliced Bread.

Their advice may very likely be at odds with mine. It is fine to listen to them as closely as you listen to me or anyone else. Above all else, make up your own mind for your own reasons: but be quick to admit your mistakes. I have a storage room at home full of mine.

Most of all, think of dive kit as a tool. We use it to have fun. Gravitate towards kit that is flexible, and don't get fixated on only one option. To believe that one type of kit is the solution to every diving challenge is to believe in a Unicorn Scenario. Diving backmount, sidemount, a CCR and even monkey style are all good in their place. Be a glutton: taste everything. You may concentrate on one style for "big dives" but don't starve opportunities to grown your experience and options by having a finicky appetite.

APPLICATION: Stage Bottles

Which brings us back to DW². A good place to start outlining the DW² approach to equipment and risk management is with stage bottles.

These are as close to ubiquitous as any other piece of kit—even closed-circuit divers use them – and rigging a stage bottle to conform to the DW² guideline is not as easy as companies selling the "store-bought" accessories for rigging them would have us believe.

First though, a definition: the term stage bottle describes an independent scuba cylinder filled with "breathing medium" and fitted with at very least a regulator first and second stage. Its exact configuration and intended use goes a long way to dictating what else the bottle has attached to it and what it contains.

The list of names and uses for this "additional" gas source include:

- Deco bottle: a cylinder filled with decompression gas to help optimize off-gassing during the diver's ascent. Fitted with regulator first and second, and a medium-sized SPG on a short hose.
- Sling bottle: any scuba cylinder carried on the side and often rigged in the traditional North Florida Cave Diver's fashion as opposed to side-mounted or hard-mounted to a primary single cylinder.
- Stage bottle/stage cylinder: a cylinder usually containing bottom mix which can be "staged" (left at a strategic point) for use in either an emergency or to extend bottom time/cave penetration. Fitted with regulator first and second, an SPG on a short hose, and occasionally a LP inflator hose with a universal Schrader connection.
- Buddy bottle: a cylinder of bottom mix used as a redundant gas source to be used in the case of an Out of Air Emergency or primary regulator failure, or other situations traditionally dealt with by signaling "share air" to a buddy. Required kit in the case of recreational solo divers. Fitted with regulator first and second, and an SPG on a short hose.
- Bailout Cylinder or Cylinders: typically an open-circuit alternative for rebreather divers in the event of a catastrophic unit failure such as a completely flooded loop or carbon-dioxide break-through. Fitted with regulator first stage and often connected directly to the diver's bailout regulator. Sometimes fitted with a standard second stage on a medium-length or long hose, and an SPG on a short hose or a button SPG.
- Contingency bottle/cylinder: Usually a pre-staged cylinder used in the event of system failure, and typically employed in complex ascents requiring multiple gas chances. Often attached to a decompression station and possibly fitted with more than one second stage.
- Redundant gas source: Another name for a Buddy Bottle, Bailout Cylinder, and Contingency Bottle.

There are probably others but this list presents the most common variants you are likely to come across.

One additional note: Many divers believe aluminum (or aluminium) alloy cylinders make great stage, bailout, deco, etc. bottles. The reasoning behind this are the buoyancy characteristics of aluminum bottles compared to steel.

CHECK OUT BUOYANCY AND TRIM IN YOUR STAGES

The classic aluminum 80 (nominally holding 80 cubic feet of "ideal gas" at its working pressure of 3000 psi and termed an 11 litre tank in the metric world). It weighs roughly 14.5 kilograms / 32 pounds on the surface when empty; but in the water in the same state has a buoyant lift of close to one and a half kilos / three and a quarter pounds (in other words, it floats when empty, and can do so even taking into account the effect of an attached regulator). When filled, the same tank has an apparent in-water weight a little more than one kilo / close to three pounds, due to the mass of the gas it is filled with.

A steel cylinder with an imperial volume of 80 cubic feet (10 litre with 230 bar working pressure) is more compact, which lends it very different characteristics in and out of the water. For example, it has thinner walls and surprisingly perhaps, less mass. A steel 80 weighs approximately 13.5 kilos /28 pounds on the surface when empty.

In the water its smaller dimensions mean it displaces less water, and when empty has an apparent in-water weight of about 1.4 kilos or three pounds. When full, that apparent weight in water is around four kilos or nine pounds. The difference between an aluminum and a similar capacity steel cylinders' buoyant shift appeals to those of us who intend to carry a bottle throughout the whole dive.

The secret to keeping sidemounted cylinders high and tight is the bungee loop (shown here on a Hollis SMS75 harness). This old-school or Armadillo-style shock-cord loop is favored by many experienced sidemount divers.

Steel bottles however, are popular when the practice or environment suggests dumping it (staging it) at the beginning of a dive. Typically, the majority of cave divers stage their decompression gas somewhere near the cave entrance at the beginning of the dive: although not all cave divers use steel decompression cylinders!

In the vast majority of diving undertaken by open-circuit technical divers, the most common uses of additional cylinders are to carry decompression gas(es) (deco bottles) and to help extend bottom time or penetration in caves (stage bottles). These can be rigged and configured in very much the same way; and the same methods and technique works for their buddies diving closed-circuit equipment, and needing to carry bailout cylinders.

A popular method is to use store-bought stage kits. These consist of a couple of bolt snaps on a long piece of webbing or rope with a loop to go over the tank valve at one end. The whole contraption is secured by a metal pipe clamp near the foot of the cylinder. The advantage of this simple design is that it is easy to find rigging kits, which are available from various mainstream equipment manufacturers. Many dive stores, even those who do not "cater" to technical divers, seem to have one or two kits in stock or on display.

Fitting this type of rigging on a stage bottle is the work of a few minutes and it effectively and quickly attaches the stage bottle reasonably close to the diver when she clips the top bolt-snap to a D ring on her shoulder harness and the bottom snap to another D ring on her hip. There is one modification to a store-bought a stage-bottle kit that will help with clipping and unclipping the bottle, as well as help it to sit as close as possible to the diver. This is to make the distance from the clip on the bottle's neck to the anchor point of the tail clip, correspond to the distance between the diver's shoulder and left hip d-rings.

However, there is one issue that a growing number of divers have with this technique: even when rigged according to Hoyle, the orientation of the stage bottle is somewhat awkward. When the diver assumes a horizontal trim, the tank's nose points down and its bum sticks in the air. A concern with this orientation particularly in tight spots, is that the business-end of the tank – the part with the valve and gas supply system attached – is likely to drag in silt or get tangled in line.

Another option is to sidemount stage bottles.

Rigging a stage for sidemount carry requires a little more planning, and the following list of accessories.

- A CAM band with steel bolt snap
- A short loop of heavy-duty bungee cord and a second steel bolt snap (a size or two smaller than the one on the CAM band)
- A plastic or silicon (preferred) snorkel keeper
- Some bungee loops or inner-tube loops for holding regulator hoses.

Let's look first at preparing the bottle itself.

Before we run through how to attach the rigging for a sidemounted stage, we need to decide on which side of our body the bottle will sit. Most divers who wish to carry a single stage, hang it on their left side. The convention for this has its genesis in old-school cave diving because of the routing of a diver's long hose from his manifold (behind his head and connecting a set of twin tanks) down the right side of his body and across his chest. That being the case, here's a step-by-step guide on how to rig a stage that will sit on the diver's left flank.

Step one: You will need a tank fitted with a valve with the orientation of the hand-wheel to the mouth of the valve on the opposite side to "normal." With the valve opening of a conventional valve facing the viewer, its hand-wheel (the on-off knob) points to the viewer's left. The majority of single tanks are fitted with left valves regardless of whether they are DIN, Yoke or Convertible. The reason usually given for this – apocryphal or otherwise – is that a right-handed diver using this valve on her back-mounted single cylinder can reach the valve behind her head [and operate it] with her right hand. In any event, for our present application – a stage on our left side – we want the other one!

Step two: Stand the tank on the floor, and look at it from above imagining an analog clock face superimposed over it. Now with the hand-wheel at 12 o'clock, the valve's mouth should point to our right, a full 90 degrees from the hand-wheel, or to three o'clock. When the tank is being carried on a dive, we want the hand-wheel to point away from our body.

This orientation will allow us to operate the valve (which may be handy if we have to feather it for some reason... see below). Also, when we are horizontal in the water, we want to have the regulator first and second stages pointing down. This is the orientation that protects the regulators, while being the most comfortable and offering the best line of sight on the reg's first stage and hoses.

Step three: Slip the CAM band over the top of the cylinder and orient the anchor point for its bolt snap to five o'clock. Now slide the CAM band down until its bottom is a few centimeters / inches from the floor. (The photo here shows the anchor point for the bottom bolt snap oriented to a 7 o'clock position; however the CAM band has not been pushed down to its final position.)

Configured this way, when the stage bottle is attached to the diver, potential line traps are as tucked away as practical.

Step four: Pull one loop of the silicon snorkel keeper over the valve so that it lays flat against the top of the cylinder with the other loop in a position that allows for the regulator mouthpiece to be stuffed into it.

Step five: Pull the small loop of thick equipment line with a bolt snap tied into it over the valve making sure it cannot slip off easily. This bolt snap will not be keeping the top of the stage bottle in place. That's the job of the bungee loop that should be fitted to the diver's harness. This bolt snap is a backup and therefore, can have some slop without effecting how tightly the tank sits to the diver's side.

Step six: slip a couple of snoopy loops or store-bought tank bands onto the tank to hold regulator hoses in place.

Step seven: Make fine adjustments to the "height" of the CAM band in the water with the help of a friend. The aim is to adjust the anchor point until the bottle sits parallel to the body's centerline with the business end not restricting the diver's arm movement. It may not be intuitive, but decreasing the distance from the anchor point of the bottom bolt snap and the bottom of the cylinder (moving the CAM band away from the valve), will push the top of the cylinder into the diver's armpit, which may not be a comfortable feeling!

FEATHERING: simple and no Secret-Agent Skills needed

I mentioned orienting the valve on a stage bottle pointing away from our body so that we can operate it, specifically feather it. Feathering is a method of preserving gas in the event of a freeflow or other gas hemorrhage from the bottle. Since we are dealing with a stage bottle or deco bottle, the gas within it will be quite important! Feathering is a useful skill – perhaps mission-critical – because it means that a bottle leaking gas does not have to be turned off and abandoned. And with the bottle and regulator set up as illustrated above, the technique is very simple and can be learned in minutes.

Start with you and your stage bottle on the surface. Be in water deep enough to support the weight of your gear but shallow enough for you to stand with your head above water. Wear a mask, have your stage regulator deployed and in your mouth.

As you breathe, practice turning off the valve with your left hand a second or two before you inhalation is complete. If there is a 100 cm hose (about 40-inches) you will drain the remaining gas in the hose as you finish breathing in. Breathe out and just as you begin the inhalation phase, crack open the valve just enough to get gas. Repeat. When you get into the rhythm, you will see the SPG needle show drop and rise in time with your breath cycles. Once you get it, still in shallow water, put your head under and try it wet. Once that's mastered, practice while swimming. When the process is really fluid, have your buddy keep the second-stage purge button depressed to simulate a freeflow while you practice.

I have seldom had second-stage freeflows but most have been from cylinders containing decompression gas. Using this method, I have completed a lengthy staged decompression from 21 metres / about 70 feet to the surface following the original schedule. My buddy and I were able to stay together and I surfaced having used only slightly more gas than he did.

I recently read a post on an online forum where someone suggested feathering a valve was unnecessarily complex and a James Bond move. He admitted he had never tried it, and offered advice because he had thought long and hard about it.

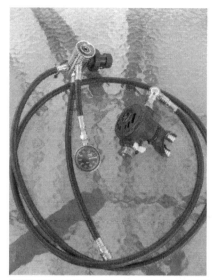

The fact is that feathering a tank valve on a sidemounted cylinder is neither complex nor a technique used by MI5 agents. If it were, I suspect students who master the technique would earn a secret decoder ring as a prize. They do not, but they do walk away with a valuable skill in my opinion.

REGULATORS FOR STAGE BOTTLES

Speaking of regulators. Once the stage bottle is configured, we probably want to get at the gas it contains. Stage regulators are very simple to configure, but we can make them a little more streamlined, and remove a couple of failure points by using some common sense.

One of the author's HOG D1 regulator sets with rotating first-stage turret. This one is set up for the right-hand cylinder when sidemount diving.

First, the quality and design of the regulator itself.

Piston, diaphragm, balanced, unbalanced? Some divers use lower-end regulators on cylinders that are used to deliver decompression gas. The argument is that these regulators are asked to perform at shallower depths. While this may be true, they are asked to perform for a long time when one is decompressing.

Typically, the ascent schedule following a dive to 60 metres, for example, will be about twice the bottom-time. So 30 minutes on the bottom, 60 breathing decompression regulators. A cheap knock off manufactured who knows where and under dodgy QA guidelines is not the smart option.

An alternative is to find a regulator that works well at apex depths and in tough environments, and use that brand or type for EVERY bottle taken into the water. This can guarantee top performance, and certainly simplifies life for the service technician.

While this can be an expensive solution, stage bottles are part of a total life-support system and the money will be invested well. (For the record, my choice is to use high performance over-balanced diaphragm first stages, some with swivel turrets, some fixed, from Hollis and HOG, on virtually all my bottles.)

At one point – following a common practice – many technical divers used unbalanced piston regulators for shallow decompression bottles. The thinking was that being unbalanced made them easier to service and repair in the field. In addition, an unbalanced regulator gives some warning when gas levels get low.

A snorkel keeper is a simple, cheap and effective method of holding a second-stage in place. The button SPG further reduces clutter on one of author's bailout cylinders.

I prefer proper gas management and an SPG to monitor gas levels, and no longer have unbalanced regulators in my OC kit.

So, let's say you have your favorite first and second stage and you want to use them on a deco or stage bottle. First the length of the LP hose connecting the two of them needs to be long enough to route it neatly when deployed but short enough to stow easily when being carried. For most applications, a 100 cm or 40-inch hose works well. The hose can be routed from the bottle around the back of the diver's neck and come into the user's mouth from the right (the traditional direction). If you are tempted to use a short hose across your chest from left to right, with its LP hose configured to attach to the second stage on the opposite side to "normal" that's fine. But consider that if you take the regulator out of your mouth, it must be clipped off immediately, or held onto, otherwise it will hang like a pendulum below your body line. Also, when swimming through any restriction, hoses routed across a diver's chest are more subject to entanglement or being pulled from the diver's mouth. This can be hugely inconvenient when navigating a restriction!

A couple more tips and suggestions. Many folks use a bolt snap tied to the business end of the LP hose near the second stage, and clip it somewhere close to the first stage to help keep things neat. I often use snorkel keepers for the same purpose. Either way works. The snorkel method does make emergency deployment a little quicker, and that may offer this method a slight advantage over the other.

Also, I do not bend HP short hoses in the shape of a U and tie it up with string or a bungee in a bid to orient the SPG on top of the first stage. It unnecessarily contorts a piece of kit exacerbating an existing potential failure point. I was taught to do it before I realised the practice effectively reduced the functional life expectancy of the hose to that of a cheap umbrella in an English winter rain storm. I got tired of replacing the rotten little things.

I think the practice of bending short hoses has its genesis in the Traditional North Florida Caver stage bottle configuration with the first stage hanging several centimetres below the diver's body line. In that orientation, perhaps tucking something as vulnerable as an SPG is the right choice. I have come to regard it though as a classic Band-Aid solution. Distorting a hose does not fix any "problem" it simply deals with a symptom. The whole issue goes away by leaving a 15 cm / six-inch hose as is and in traditional SM style, having it pointing towards the diver's shoulder. In this position, it can be seen, is protected and is much less likely to volunteer as a line trap.

An alternative is to point the hose back down the cylinder body so that the SPG sits against the cylinder walls. This is really only recommended on stage bottles where gas levels are checked infrequently.

DSMB: Your alternative buoyancy device

Diving with too much ballast is dangerous and has been a trigger in many fatal dive events. Notwithstanding this, many beginning divers carry too much ballast, and many instructors make it that way in a bid to make their job "easier" because their classes are conducted with everyone kneeling on the bottom of the pool. However, sport divers more than any other divers should be 'weighted' correctly.

The standard test is when dressed to dive, wear a cylinder containing 50 bar of gas (imperial divers use 500 – 600 psi). With no gas in the BCD, a diver should be able to hold his or her position at the surface floating at eye-level with moderately full lungs. They begin to sink when they exhale. For a technical or advanced diver, things are not as simple.

To begin with, an advanced or technical diver's cylinders should never be that empty! A better starting point is to do a similar test with one-third of the starting gas volume in the main cylinders. If decompression or stage bottles are going to be used on the dive, these should also be worn but these can be close to empty (at which point, they will have a tendency to float).

At the beginning of her dive, the average technical diver is overweighed. The issue is the quality of gas she and her buddies will be carrying for their "mission." Gas has mass. It is not uncommon for the volume of gas used during a technical dive and consequent decompression to add more than seven kilos (15 pounds or so) to a diver's weight at the beginning of the dive.

This presents some special problems... potentially. The term "Balanced Kit" is used to describe any kit configuration – traditional doubles, sidemount, CCR et al – that the diver is able to "swim" back to the surface from depth should he or she suffer a catastrophic failure in their primary buoyancy device (usually a wing or SM harness with integrated wing).

Unlike most sport divers, few open-circuit technical divers have any or much truly ditchable weight. Their ballast is supplied by integral items of kit such as steel primary cylinders and a stainless-steel backplate. Sidemount divers may have the option of dropping one primary cylinder if needed, but divers wearing back-mounted doubles do not.

In either case though, a diver begins a technical dive over-weighted if measured using the ruler we'd use for the same diver doing a sport dive. In the event of a wing failure, however unlikely, there has to be some back-up strategy to get back to the surface uninjured.

When considering buoyancy and specifically risk management and buoyancy, an advanced or technical diver might consider their kit as falling into four categories.

- Those items subject to significant buoyancy shift, either controlled or uncontrolled (such as scuba cylinders, wing or BCD, drysuit, wetsuit and a lift bag or delayed surface marker buoy)
- Those with a 'non-variable' buoyant nature (such as the diver, floaty fins, a camera or other accessories)
- Permanent ballast: items that sink and are not detachable (such as a backplate and primary back-mounted cylinders, harness hardware, regulators, and so on)
- Ditchable ballast: items that sink but which can be dumped (for example, this might include heavy canister lights, stage bottles (when full), weight belt, reels, and in extreme circumstances, one steel cylinder for a sidemount diver).

Understanding and classifying your personal dive gear along these guidelines, one can begin to build a set of acceptable actions if the world ever goes pear-shaped.

For example, you could find answers to the following questions. What would be the possible first moves if your inflation hose and wing became separate entities? How many items of ballast can you remove from your standard kit? At the beginning of a dive, when one can get back "home" without any decompression obligation and the need to switch gas, dropping a stage or two can make swimming to the surface possible and easier. Is that an option for you?

Think and list what alternatives you have to help overcome gravity? The increased buoyancy from a drysuit can, in some cases, provide enough lift to replace a broken wing.

USE AVAILABLE AIDS TO HELP STABILIZE YOURSELF

Here are some other options. If there is structure nearby – a wall, a shelf, a wreck, whatever — use it to stabilize yourself. Grab it, get yourself sorted out, "talk" the situation through with your buddy and try to relax. (Have respect for the environment but when the alternative is disappearing into the abyss, grab on.) Unless your wing failure was accompanied by a huge loss of gas from your cylinder, you have something to breathe while you think. Relax and work out your options.

If there is no structure to support you, grab your buddy and use them as a stabilizer. It's surprisingly simple to hang onto a buddy's harness and let them add a little additional gas to their wing to support the two of you. Unless the pair of you are grossly over-weighted, one technical wing can support two divers in the water wearing balanced kit. But it does require a little practice, and is much easier to accomplish with style when part of a three-person team!

If there is an upline, make for it and use it. At this point it may be worth noting that a Prusik knot or Prusik loop (shown here) can be useful place to hang from while you work on options. A Prusik is simple to tie to an upline and can be used just as effectively as an ascender is used in rock climbing (their original application).

To tie a Prusik knot you need what climbers call "Prusik slings," which are lengths of thin cord. Climbers use 5mm or 6mm diameter line but for work in water, a thinner cord works fine. In fact, the thinner the cord is in relation to the thickness of the anchor line, the greater the ability of the knot to cinch onto the rope.

Make Prusik slings about 70 cm / two feet long. Tie the ends together with a double-fisherman's knot, forming a closed loop.

The first step to tie a Prusik knot is to keep the loop's knot in your hand. Then, take the loop of cord behind the climbing rope and bring half of the loop through the other half of the loop and form a girth hitch. A girth hitch is a basic knot for attaching a sling or cord to any object, including a tree, piece of climbing gear, or, in this case, an anchor line. Bring the loop of cord back through the girth hitch on the upline two to three more times, forming a barrel with the tail of the cord hanging out from the middle. This is simply done by wrapping the loop of cord through the inside of each previous wrap. After you're done wrapping the rope, tighten the knot and dress it by carefully arranging all the wraps of cord so they lie next to each other and not crossed.

How many wraps of cord you put on the knot is up to you. Usually two will hold several staged cylinders in place.

I carry a length of 3 mm sling in my wetNotes for this reason.

Your options should be golden with a combination of a solid upline, a drysuit, removable ballast, a prussic loop, plus the administrations of your buddy. But what if there is no upline.

This would be a good time to send a Delayed Surface Marker Buoy (DSMB) aloft. Depending on how your surface support has been briefed, it may be prudent to deploy a surface marker even if there is an upline. With the exception of the very smallest, silliest "safety sausage," a DSMB (by the way, the delayed tacked on the front of its name is because it is only deployed at the end of a dive) should provide sufficient lift to support a diver in place of a wing. If you have the choice, you may prefer to hang from a line attached to a small cavern or wreck reel rather than a spool in this situation, but either works just fine; and spools rarely jam or bird's nest.

There are several designs available. There are DSMBs which have a self-sealing end. Gas is added via an open bottom, which unlike a traditional lift bag, is effectively a one-way valve. A second type has a device that fits into the standard Schrader valve on the end of LP inflation hoses. Yet a third offers both options, and a fourth has a small gas cylinder attached, which inflates the buoy when it is cranked open.

All four types should also be fitted with an operational over-pressure dump to prevent expanding gas from splitting the bag open on its way to the surface. More important than any debate over which version is the best, is that every diver is proficient in using and deploying it properly.

Properly in this instance means that the marker buoy arrives on the surface full and capable of providing its rated lift, and without the diver tangled in it. It is worth noting that a DSMB is designed and primarily intended to float with most of its length out of the water marking the position of the diver. When it's being used as a buoyancy aid, most of it will be submerged.

Which does warrant the question, how much lift can a DSMB give? Of course, that depends on how big they are and what volume of water they displace when full. I have four or five different models and the only common thing about the buoyancy rating for each one is how inaccurate the manufacturer's ratings are.

The best way to calculate how much lift a particular buoy is going to deliver is to fill it with water and weigh it (using a luggage scale or electronic fish scale) or measure it with a measuring jug.

For example, the smallest DSMB I own, weighs a couple of hundred grams (a few ounces) when it's empty. Not really much of a factor. When it is full of water, it weighs a little more than six kilograms, which means it is capable of delivering six kilos of lift. (I am sure you can use a similar method with pounds and cubic feet and gallons, but honestly, it's easier using metric units).

My largest, a monstrous contraption that stands taller than I am, is capable of offering more than 25 kilos / 55 pounds of lift! A marker buoy this size is too big to weigh on a fish scale (hauling it up by its end would likely cause its seams to burst). It was weighed using a bathroom scale.

When you buy your first DSMB, I suggest testing its buoyancy and making a mental note, or writing your results in indelible marker near the inflator.

If you do not already own a luggage scale, fish scale or digital bathroom scales, you can get as good results by simply measuring how many litres of water the DSMB holds. Since one litre of water weighs one kilogram, your DSMB will offer a kilo of lift for every litre of water it holds. (There is a slight variation from salt to fresh water, but frankly, for these calculations, not enough to worry about.)

In several thousand dives, I have had one wing failure and one instance of a buddy experiencing a complete wing failure. I have conducted a couple of test dives with the dump valve removed from my wing – just for the fun of it – but only one real-world failure. Therefore, the weight of logic and statistical evidence is on their side of the argument that states that this type of gear failure is highly unlikely. The chances are it will never happen to you at any time.

However, next time you have a dive planned with your usual buddies at a site with a hard bottom within sensible distance of the surface, and you have nothing better to do, try this. Empty your wing completely and get yourself back to the surface using an alternative method. You will certainly learn something about yourself and possibly the folks you dive with, and most likely you'll have fun too.

DOUBLE BLADDER

A few manufacturers make wings and SM harnesses with "dual" or redundant bladders. I am not a fan of these for several reasons. Firstly, in the event of a puncture (something I have never encountered on a dive, so take my advice with that in mind) it seems logical that whatever was capable of putting a hole in one's primary bladder is also capable of doing a similar number on the backup.

An argument might be made that a dual or double-bladder wing does provide back-up if the primary inflator hose breaks off completely or the dump valve leaks. I believe that with a thorough pre-dive inspection both these surprises can be almost completely eliminated, and that a leaking dump valve is not a major issue at all.

I also find the second inflator hose that double-bladder systems have is awkward, and it takes up valuable real-estate I'd rather have for more useful kit.

However, let me explain the major concern with this type of gear. A potential danger with any BCD, wing or harness is a run-away ascent triggered by a LP inflator freeflow. This is an "emergency" we deal with by either quickly disconnecting the LP hose or turning off the tank to which it's connected... or both.

This is something we drill for and which is usually a minor inconvenience. There have been a couple of deaths and several injuries as a result of divers suffering run-away ascents when wearing double bladder wings with BOTH inflators connected. They were injured after they disconnected or turned off the wrong hose in the rush that followed the free flow. By the time they realized their mistake, they were heading for the surface.

Therefore, if you insist on wearing a dual-bladder wing or harness, I suggest strongly that you only have one LP hose connected to it. A total wing failure is a rare happening. Judicious handling during transportation, a good assembly and pre-dive inspection, and a bubble-check before descending can all help prevent this particular failure. On the other hand, a freeflow from a faulty Schrader valve is a possibility and a potential killer if it cannot be controlled.

That said, losing a wing at depth would be serious, and in most cases could really ruin your day. I believe the best solution to the threat is to carry a good-sized DSMB and spool and practice its use just in case.

A RECAP

So, let's recap quickly. Risk management extends to Equipment, which is a bit of a moving target because of changes in use and trends in the marketplace (take the growth of sidemount as an example). The overall approach of DW^2 is to understand that kit configuration – although a factor in managing risk – is of lesser importance than, say component design and QA.

One small proviso. The DW^2 "rules" around kit selection may seem more flexible than other approaches, but do conform to the Hogarthian suggestion (see the full explanation at the end of this chapter), that kit and your mindset need to be appropriate. In some cases, one may need to accommodate some level of compromise; however, compromise should never be allowed to affect safety negatively. One has to draw the line somewhere.

Here is a "for instance" about drawing a line. Recently, I was asked by a transitioning diver if he could use his Hollis sidemount rig (a popular brand sidemount harness) for doubles and a single back-mounted cylinder as well.

My answer was: you might be able too, but you really, really don't want to. I have also been asked if a diver can use a backplate and wing to dive sidemount. The answer is the same.

If you want to dive sidemount properly and make it work, the last thing you need is a backplate. A backplate is designed to offer a firm platform to hang a hoking pair of steel cylinders off. A backplate is excellent for twin cylinders, but has no useful function for carrying cylinders by one's side (which incidentally means precisely at the diver's side and not hanging in front of him looking like an after-thought.)

Running a close second in the what-you-don't-want-sweepstakes for sidemount is the wing (BCD) designed to function with that backplate and that was originally and primarily designed for doubles.

A wing intended to offer buoyant lift to someone wearing doubles offers that lift is in exactly the WRONG places for sidemount. A doubles diver (who is wearing the correct sized cylinders for their body size) usually needs lift along the length of her tanks with a little more lift around her shoulders. The same diver dressed in sidemount gear needs that lift closer to her hips in a totally different configuration.

A side view of the excellent SMS 75 (sidemount system 75) from Hollis. Note the shape of the buoyancy cell (wing) which puts lift on the hips rather than the shoulders.

Additionally, a wing or a poorly designed SM harness for that matter, will open up to look like she is wearing a huge Venus fly-trap on her back as soon as gas is added, because there is nothing (no tanks) keeping it in place. This is known as the Taco-effect. It can also be seen when a diver makes the mistake of using a wing designed for doubles with only a single tank on her back.

Maybe a very experienced SM diver could make a sidemount harness work for a set of backmounted doubles because of his or her skill, but even they would still look like a bag of hammers on a merry-go-round. It simply does not work. It is also potentially dangerous as well as unsightly.

When we analyse equipment from a risk management perspective, form does become function. When a diver's kit configuration is as disorganized as the discount video bin in Walmart, things can quickly become dangerous. In almost every case, unruly kit, poorly configured and designed to do something very different to what it is being asked to do, will defy quick deployment, will make fine control difficult or impossible, and will perform sub-optimally. It may easily make a small issue worse and contribute to confusion and a poor outcome.

In other words, a SM harness is for sidemount and it will simply be too much of a compromise to work with anything else. NOW looking around at various submissions on YouTube, it apparent that all sorts of people will disagree with me, but sidemount – or traditional North Florida Cave kit for that matter – requires one to pick gear specifically designed to be used in the context of that specific configuration style.

The take-home message is this: I can fry you an egg on the back of a plasterer's trowel but an omelet pan works better.
And for general SM use, a Hollis SMS75 is a clear front-runner over any wing on any stainless steel or aluminum backplate,
even one from Hollis.

A FINAL NOTE

In the grand scheme of things, and with some rather obvious exceptions – for example, having to bailout at 110 metres to a non-functioning OC second-stage regulator with a torn diagram – equipment failure offers little to no threat. To paraphrase Bill Main: equipment failure is unlikely to kill you; but your reaction to it most certainly could.

What seems to cause divers at all levels and from all diving categories the most grief is the potential cascade or domino effect. Something small breaks and in the process of dealing with that issue, a diver suddenly realizes he is unable to access the thing that backs up that piece of kit or that fixes the issue its breaking presents.

Recently, a diver died at a popular central-Florida dive site. A laundry-list of mistakes and poor decisions was made worse because his buddy's spare regulator (octopus) was trapped under a BC strap and inaccessible.

Alarmingly often, it is the smallest and seemingly most trivial thing that triggers a fatal event. Things like a broken mask strap, a knot slipping undone, a regulator second-stage too tightly secured, a gauge obscured by other clutter; these can all be triggers that lead to harm and injury.

I cannot stress enough the advice not to over-burden yourself with kit. Be circumspect and miserly in your selection of things to take in the water with you. Things that are unlikely to break may not have to be backed up, especially if inspected and properly tested as part of a pre-dive ritual. Therefore, you may not need to carry three extra ones just because you got a dozen of them for Christmas! Most of all, pre-dive inspections, S-drills, bubble-checks, self-assessment, recognizing stress in your buddy and diving with like-minded people are simple ways to build a barrier between you and disaster.

Remember as well, it does not take much to contingency yourself out of the water, but with a little forward thinking, planning and practice, there is no need to.

COMMON PRINCIPLES: Hogarthian meets Doing What Works DW²

Cave diver and reluctant gear guru, Bill Hogarth Main, is not some fictional figure created to frighten the meek into conformity. He is just a guy who has been cave diving for a good while and, as far as I know, he still guides at a couple of select caves in North Florida: the area of the USA where he makes his home.

Hogarthian Gear Configuration is named after Bill because it is based on the minimalist approach that he popularized among cave divers before cave diving and technical diving came out of the closet. Because of this approach, Hogarthian has been referred to as the Zen of Cave Diving. Not a bad definition really since the Alpinist Way or Minimalist Approach to any active, high-stress, high-risk sport is commonly linked to the mindless-in-the-moment alpha awareness that Zen practitioners promote.

In the years since the Hogarthian concept was introduced to the wider diving community, the principles – which in the original form were VERY straightforward and abundantly clear – have been distorted and applied to concepts that have, to some of us, strayed from what was originally admirably sensible, to whacked-out and weird.

With his tongue firmly in-cheek, cave explorer Larry Green coined the phrase "Doing What Works" or DW² some 20 years after the original Hogarthian concept hit the streets. He intended DW² to describe a slightly updated look at kit configuration which stuck closely to Hogarth's main tenets; including its most important: Constant focus on improving the system, because nothing is perfect.

What follows are each of the main points of the Hogarthian approach to gear choices and configuration through the DW² lens.

SIMPLE: nothing convoluted or contrived, and if something can be shaved off, filed down, or trimmed off, it is done. Nothing illustrates the call to keep things simple more than a line spool. The picture here shows a cold-water version (wider center for accommodating gloves) from Light Monkey.

Another example of simple might be a piece of kit that can be fixed properly with stuff available from a hardware store. (This was explained to me when discussing the pros and cons of the technology available for cave lights with Bill Main and Lamar English back when I had hair and cave lights were less reliable than they now are: but the idea remains sound.)

Simple also means that a diver resists any temptation to buy 'add-on' gadgets that over complicate or compromise clean design without adding function. Obviously, you can buy whatever appeals to you, but the suggestion in this approach is to avoid fussy solutions to problems that don't exist and that may introduce more potential for failure. For example, the scuba gadget equivalent of a retractable dog leash is an over-complicated solution to clipping a piece of kit like an SPG to a diver's harness. A bolt snap does the trick with less cost, takes up less real-estate, and provides a very serviceable solution with far less complication. It's also less likely to break!

SERVICED: it should be pretty easy to get this one straight. Nothing goes into the water that is not in working order. For basic life-support gear – stuff that delivers gas – serviced means gear that is checked out and serviced by a qualified technician according to guidelines published by the manufacturer, following at least the minimum service schedule suggested by that manufacturer. It also means that every piece of kit has its function fully tested before it is taken into the water. So, regulators should be test breathed while slightly submerged. Valves should be opened and closed (and opened again where appropriate); hoses and hose connections inspected for wear and tear (and replaced if showing signs of age or abuse); Schrader valves inspected and tested; seals and straps inspected and stress-tested; primary and back-up lights checked for adequate charge, and so on.

STANDARD: means that you and the other members of your dive team have agreed on the appropriate way to plan and execute your dive. Standard when it applies to kit, enables each and all team members to provide rapid help with a full understanding of what to do if something hits the fan during a dive. The guideline to standardize broadly applied, covers the attitude and mental approach of team members to the operational niceties (and limits) of the team itself as well as the equipment it will be using on their dive.

It would be easy to interpret this guideline naively and mandate brand specific, even color specific elements of kit to team members for every dive in all conditions, and ignore innovation, new options and better solutions.

This is not, in my opinion, in the spirit of the original concept and certainly not DW². While it might be simple and less bother to suggest that everyone follows the leader no questions asked, this approach is far from optimal, and certainly does not encourage questions or allow for innovation.

If the technical diving community has learned anything during the past 20 years or so, it is surely that the process of gear design, gear selection and gear configuration is one of evolution – triggered perhaps by small revolutions, but essentially a constantly developing slow progression of ideas and methods based on best practice. And best practice is by definition and application, anything but static.

In part, this is perhaps why the definition of Standard in the context of a Hogarthian or DW² approach is the most fluid and difficult to pin down. For example, as I write this, it seems to me that the ubiquitous canister light – the "standard" primary light for technical and cave divers for a generation – is becoming an outdated technology with too many potential failure points to warrant its use on critical dives.

Several handheld lights are less bulky than the current standard, have no chord to manage, have fewer failure points, are just as powerful and have workable burn times compared to canister lights that retail at more than five times their price.

SHARED: means that in essence, your buddy has your six-o'clock (your backside if you are unfamiliar with analog time-pieces). This principle can be applied to most of what is taken into the water and certainly ALL of what is essential. The Fundamental thing shared though is breathing gas. Technical divers follow gas rules that dictate that a portion of the gas in YOUR tanks belongs to your buddy.

This concept is at the core of team diving and technical diving especially. Here's the basic rule: As technical divers on open-circuit equipment, we are conditioned from our earliest technical training onward to carrying extra gas – one-third of our starting volume is for our buddy, and half of the deco gas we have with us, is for sharing with our buddy in an emergency.

These rules are sacrosanct: no reasonable dive plan would suggest compromising the margin of safety offered by these basic gas management guidelines. And they extend to closed-circuit gas planning too. CCR divers routinely carry gas which, in the case of a serious malfunction, is for themselves or may be shared with a buddy.

And the shared philosophy extends to other things beside gas.

Perhaps the most important and most easily ignored and first to be overlooked is that we share the responsibility to plan our dives! In addition, we share the work of carrying additional gear needed on dives, and we share the role of mother hen while looking out for the well-being and safe return of our fellow team members.

Shared is simply a basic and fundamental necessity in this type of diving.

SUITABLE: if a piece of kit was never intended or designed to cope with the dive environment, resist the urge to force the issue. Pushing the functional envelope of a piece of kit is what test divers are paid to do; and then only in controlled conditions.

It needs to be pointed out that when a diver does a "suitability-check" it should be applied critically to every component of his or her kit. A common mistake, and one that opens a diver up to potentially serious grief, is stop analysing when the life-support systems and gas choices check out.

Of course these are critically important. Will this regulator perform at depth; is this the right mix for this dive; is there enough life left in the scrubber to keep me safe if something happens and I have to spend longer in the water than planned. However, checking for suitability must cover more.

Let me give you an example. When I dive CCR, at least one of my bailout bottles is usually connected through the unit's manifold directly into the system that feeds my OCB (Open-Circuit Bailout).

According to one level of analysis, this bottle does not need to be fitted with a traditional second-stage. However, because I dive as part of a team, I have to consider the potential of sharing the gas it contains with a buddy.

I may have to donate the gas in that bottle at some point on the way back to fresh air. Until recently, I had a short hose (about 60 cm or 24 inches) on that second stage. Doing drills with students, it was apparent that that length hose was inconveniently short. It was in essence, unsuitable.

In the final push, when there are doubts about the suitability of a particular piece of kit for a dive – even something as seemingly minor as the length of a hose – the best action is to replace it with something that is known to work: a longer hose, a better first-stage, warmer thermal togs, a hood that fits, no matter what.

STREAMLINED: now this particular suggestion should come as no surprise to anyone who has read any book on technical diving. Short version: do not look like a Christmas tree! Tuck away or completely get rid of things that dangle. Aim for minimal resistance when swimming. (I was once called on this score by Bill Main for wearing a drysuit to go cave diving. But when you think about streamlining in the fullest sense, a baggy, telescopic trilaminate drysuit – even one that retails for several thousand dollars – does have the potential to create drag in a medium 800 times denser than air.)

Streamlined equipment is important to alleviate stress and task-loading !. In a way, streamlining goes hand-in-hand with suitable, shared and simple: if it's possible to leave it behind do so.

From time-to-time I have had students ask if they can bring a camera with them on training dives. With the advent of tiny digital models such as Go-Pro, the default answer (No!) is under review... depending on the dive.

At some point, the definition Hogarthian got high-jacked because people started to apply it to kit choices and configurations that were the width of many city blocks away from what started out as a good idea. Hence the birth of DW^2.

There is certainly nothing wrong with progress. Smart innovations in industrial design, electronic engineering, and materials manufacturing have made fools out of many of us who said: "I'll never do that!" But I am not sure that moving away from the six basics guidelines that originally defined Hogarthian Configuration, and that now form the basis of DW^2, constitutes good thinking or best practice.

In other words, DW^2, Hogarthian, or whatever flavor of "Kit-Konfiguration-Kool-Aid" is in favor with your local dive community, most certainly cannot be the perfect solution. Everything embraces at very least a touch of compromise. But as long as it's not abundantly stupid or dangerous, it will do until something better comes along. Just be aware that regardless of how many badges of belonging you have, when it comes to dive gear, something safer, more reliable, better always does come along: you just need to be ready to accept it.

Chapter Eight

OPERATIONS

In the context of dive planning, operations is a term used to describe the final step in the eight-part risk management strategy. Operations incorporates three equally important sub-processes. I have seen them written as: Plan the dive; Dive the Plan; Discuss the Plan.

In some settings – less so in recreational diving than say commercial, public safety, scientific or military diving – the word operations is replaced by the initials S-O-P (Standing Operating Procedures or when the procedures apply across a broad spectrum of applications, Standard Operating Procedures).

For example, in commercial diving, SOP (pronounced as a string of letters) is a set of detailed, written, step-by-step instructions put in place to make sure the required level of uniform performance is maintained for each of the specific tasks that has to be carried out leading up to, during and after the dive.

SOPs would usually define the selection, inspection and preparation of equipment; the training, experience, and fitness of people selected to complete tasks relating to the dive; and the standing or standard methodology and metrics employed to achieve and assess results.

Essentially, an SOP is an extremely detailed dive plan that carefully and completely explains the appropriate "best practice" to arrive at a desired end result.

Here's a tiny extract from the 13-page Surface Supply SOPs for U.S. Government work:

3.4.4 Gas Supply Manifold Block

The diver's harness-mounted manifold block typically has two ports for attachment of incoming gas supply, one port for the dry suit inflator hose, one port for attachment of the breathing regulator, and two low pressure ports for auxiliary equipment. The primary incoming port is for attachment of the umbilical breathing gas line. This port must have a functioning non-return valve to ensure that a loss of umbilical line pressure, combined with depth pressure, won't suck the gas out of the diver's lungs or out of the emergency gas supply tank. This ensures that in the event of umbilical air supply loss, the diver will receive air from the emergency gas supply (EGS). Prior to attaching the umbilical hose to the manifold block, the non-return valve should be tested by blowing into the valve (air should flow freely through the valve), and then sucking on the valve (no air should come back through the valve).

Clearly, this kind of intense detail is over the top for most of us, and for most of the dives we undertake for pleasure. It would be impractical to attempt anything close to the level of control (and reporting) mandated when dive operations are expected to follow industrial or governmental policies and guidelines.

I cannot imagine any recreational diver bothering to pull out a 13-page SOP to ensure his shallow bimble to try out a new pair of fins is "done by the book." However, there are several valuable lessons we can pinch from the SOP concept. Certainly it should be easy to see the latent benefits that a structured SOP-type document could bring to complex and involved adventures.

We'll look at a portion of an SOP designed for diving later. But be warned if you do decide to adopt a more structured approach to your "big" dives by applying some level of operations management including the use of an SOP, the habit tends to trickle down and tint the preparations for more simple dives: sometimes even to the simplest; such as a dip in the local quarry to test new kit.

STEP ONE: Plan the Dive
Above all else, technical diving is a team activity. The two-buddy system works OK for sport diving – that is when situational awareness is present and both buddies understand what's expected of them and have the skills to execute correctly.

Technical diving often goes more smoothly with teams of three or multiples of two or three working as a unit. In other words, if you and I were diving with my friend Erik, each of us would have a redundant buddy: two buddies each in case one of them "breaks." If you and your buddy dive with me and Erik, we dive as four people divided into two teams of two; and I have one buddy and two redundant buddies just in case Erik breaks. If you and I go diving with three friends, we have each other as a buddy and if one of us breaks, we can borrow the "spare" buddy from the three-some diving with us. And so it goes. There is a limit to how large a group can function as a unit – for example, when filming, eight (a 3-3-2 formation) is about it for me – but regardless of the team's size and what internal formation it takes, the team ethos should always rule.

The team concept can also extend to those left on the surface. In the case of boat diving, this includes, at a minimum, the captain and crew. In many circumstances, and to avoid the ever-present threat cast by potential litigation, charter boat staffers often stress to their customers that their only obligation is to provide a lift to and from the dive site. This may be the case but even so, the boat crew are going to be "first responders" in the case of something going pear-shaped before, during or after your dive. At very least, make them aware of your dive plan, your planned bottom time and whether things like the sudden appearance of a delayed surface marker buoy part-way through the dive indicates a problem or not.

Most of my diving, the vast majority of my diving, involves a couple of buddies. I am used to teams of three divers. It's an easy and effective formation. However, I have dived as part of, and occasionally led much larger teams, which included support divers, whose job it was to help keep everyone safe while wet, as well as additional surface personnel who watched out for everyone getting into our out of the water.

This type of diving adds levels of complication and obligation that many divers will find unacceptable. Often, highly complex dives carried out by a large team require an operations manager or a 'diving officer.' This person's responsibility is to oversee diver safety, ensure protocols and procedures are followed, orchestrate who gets into the water when, keep records and, in the event of a mishap, take charge of the response. It's their show and they run it.

Admittedly, titles such as diving officer, support diver, and surface support, and images of people waiting on the surface with clipboards and stop watches, move us away from purely recreational and into the realm of expedition diving – which is well beyond the scope of this book – but the management of operations, even for mundane outings with our mates at a well-known dive site, have many things in common with the challenges of full-blown expedition dives at remote sites a long way from home.

For example: the question of how to coordinate the activities of a group, when that group includes more than a couple of people is a common challenge. The essential skill of getting a group to function as a unit is communications. Communications within the group is essential, whether the group consists of two people or twenty. Communications at all phases of the dive from planning through debriefing is also essential. My experience is that as the number of people involved in a dive increases, the things that can be taken for granted decreases.

Now unless you hang out with folks who are enthusiastic clairvoyants and skilled mind-readers (in which case write to me about your experiences… your mates know the address), by far the simplest way to achieve communication, symmetry of purpose, and faultless execution is to start things off with a group conversation.

Robert Copeland, wrote: *To get something done, a committee should consist of no more than three [people], two of whom are absent.* Anyone who has volunteered time to a festival, fundraiser, or community event will probably agree with Copeland, but technical diving is about more persuasive issues than who's going to bake two dozen butter tarts for the church social or who should play Mabel in the Rotary Club's staging of *The Pirates of Penzance* next Christmas.

Also, because everyone has to accept the risks involved in diving, and the responsibilities of working in a team, there has to be buy-in from all.

The actual risks involved in an activity may or may not be relative to experience and equipment, but the perception of those risks is absolutely relative and personal to every individual diver. Because of this, everyone involved in a dive not matter how insignificant the risk may seem to you or me, should have an opportunity to comment, sanction, suggest, and veto. I've witnessed divers (and teams of divers) who believe a form of dictatorship is the better way to get results. Copeland's advice notwithstanding, you'll find that even a benevolent dictatorship tends to discourage true team-building, and stifles a free exchange of new ideas and creative solutions. A directed democracy gets the sort of results that simply never occur when a group's imagination is subordinated to one person's knowledge, experience and ego.

However, we have to recognize that there are times and circumstances where getting agreement from a half-dozen people will be like herding cats. Sometimes, someone or something has to take the initiative; and that's where an unpretentious form of Standing Operating Procedures is handy.

Let's begin with a simple SOP, something generic enough to use as a base for almost every dive we are likely to do. Something we can bolt additional protocols on to as needed when the complexity of our dives warrants more foresight and control.

First though, a mission statement. The primary mission of all technical dives is that everyone, each diver, all members of the team, finish the dive in no worse shape or in even better shape than when it began. Safety is always the first and most essential priority. Safety surpasses all other considerations. And so it follows that the first items in all operational considerations, the basic blue-print for survival and success, is to protect and shelter participants from risk.

So if we were to draw up a list of items to check off as we run through our mini-SOP it might read:

1. All diving is a gamble of some sort, but do you believe your dive plan has eliminated, ameliorated or avoided risks and that the odds of success are in your favor?

2. Are you trained, equipped and ready to dive?

3. Is your buddy (are your buddies) similarly trained, equipped and ready to dive

4. Have you and your team-mates practiced skills relevant to the dive recently

5. Might environmental conditions (weather, current/tides/flow, visibility etc.) change your answers to 1, 2, 3 & 4; and if so, what alternatives/options are the safest?

6. Let someone who is not diving know your dive plan and at what time you should return. Make sure they know who or which agencies to alert if you do not return when you planned to.

7. Have a first-aid kit including medical oxygen, EMS contact information, and a printed five-minute neurological exam and water-proof notepad at your dive site.

8. Immediately before the dive gets wet, get agreement from everyone that the dive is a GO. (Remember anyone can call any dive at any time for any reason).

9. Distribute and work through gear assembly and pre-dive checklist(s) with dive buddy(ies).

    a. Assembly checklist should include inspection of all casings, hoses, o-rings and other consumables, and require that ALL regulators be wet-breathed, all buttons and dump valves tested, gases analysed and labelled, etc. (See sample checklist below).

10. Gas volume (OC): The usable volume of bottom gas for each team member will be no greater than two-thirds of smallest starting volume, preserving at least one-third for contingency use. Each team member must carry twice the volume of decompression gas needed by the team member with highest estimated SAC rate.

11. Gas Volume (CCR): Add a minimum of 25 percent to oxygen and diluent volume needs and carry these volumes as a minimum. Calculate bailout needs with initial RMV (first five minutes) at a SAC rate of 30 l/min to account for elevated breathing rates following carbon dioxide break-through.

12. Diving in a hard overhead (Cave, Wreck) requires redundant gas supply to provide a ready option in the event of primary cylinder failure (regulator, valve, o-rings etc.)

13. If a personal dive computer (PDC) is used to track decompression obligation, carry a backup computer with the same or a more conservative algorithm/settings, and/or tables created with margin of error for greater than, less than times and depth where applicable.

14. When PDCs are used, algorithm and conservatism settings must be the same throughout group. When this is impractical, whole team will follow the most conservative profile to ensure that no diver will be "left alone to finish his/her deco."

15. Emergency at Depth (protocol overview)

    a. Seven-point: Recognize a problem exists; communicate to team; Identify problem's source; consider options; enact optimal solution; co-ordinate solution with team; terminate dive.

16. Emergency on Surface (protocol overview)

    a. Eight-point: Recognize a problem exists; Establish buoyancy; communicate to team; identify problem's source; consider options; enact optimal solution; co-ordinate solution with team; get to "dry land."

17. Begin each dive with "START." S-drill, Team check, Air checks, Route confirmation, Time and Tables confirmation.

18. Identify specific WAYPOINTS/GO-GO HOME CHECKS for every dive and use them. Basic waypoints at which each team member is asked "Do we go or do we go home?" include: immediately before submersion; after six-metre S-drill; at arrival at target depth (start of gold line in cave); turn the dive (first team member has consumed controlling gas volume or agreed upon lapsed time is reached, whichever is first); arrival back at exit point/ascent line; beginning of each required decompression stops (safety stop); ascent to surface; time when each diver has shucked gear and begins SIT.

19. Conduct Post-dive Debrief and make any required changes to dive plan.

20. In effect, an SOP has to include checklists specific to the equipment being used. For example, the assembly and pre-dive checklists I use when diving my personal AP Evolution+ CCR fitted with back-mounted counter-lungs and a tech-travel frame (in addition to the electronic checklist displayed on the handset), reads as follows:

Suggested Assembly Checklist:

- Check for signs of dirt, deterioration and damage to any part of the CCR at all first stages
- Inspect o-rings and hoses
- Inspect handset, cables, electrical connections
- Check batteries have sufficient voltage for dive

o (my personal comfort zone ends when batteries deliver less than 5.2 volts).

- Check battery compartments are tightly closed
- Refill scrubber basket with Sofnolime® 797 (Non indicating)
- Lubricate basket o-ring and spacer ring
- Check lid o-ring and attach lid
- Analyze, check pressure, and install filled gas cylinders
- Install canister, blow oxygen hose clear and attach to solenoid inlet
- Secure basket in metal casing with two retaining nuts
- Check hoses, mouthpiece, verify non-return valve operation (mushroom valves)
- Use cell validator to check cells are not current limited (verify at 1.3 bar minimum)
- Attach hoses to counter-lung T-pieces
- Negative pressure test
- Turn on cylinders, pressurize lines, turn off, look for pressure drop
- Turn on cylinders
- Check inter-stage pressures (oxygen (7-7.5 bar) and diluent (8.5-9.5 bar)
- Turn on electronics, confirm all OK
- Calibrate before every dive if handset has been turned off
- Verify operation of oxygen and diluent manual addition valves
- Verify operation of automatic diluent addition valve
- Positive pressure test
- Inspect silicon mouthpiece for splits or holes. Replace if necessary.
- If not diving immediately, turn cylinders off, drain IP lines, flush breathing loop with air, and turn electronics off
- Stow carefully

Immediate Pre-Dive Checks:

- Verify all gas supplies on
- Verify gas pressures conform to dive guidelines
- Verify bailout pressure(s) and check bailout regulators by wet-breathing
- Check BC inflation and deflation
- Confirm ADV is operational
- Verify handset's checklist AND DO NOT SWITCH OFF
- Confirm correct diluent is shown on handset
- Check appropriate bailout gas is an option on handset
- Check PO2 at least 0.7 bar
- Verify mouthpiece (open/closed)
- Conduct pre-breathe and confirm temp stick responds

- Check HUD (heads-up display) is green
- Confirm PO2, check CO2 status, go dive

Although the SOP presented here may seem extensive to those of you unfamiliar with preparations for technical dives, it is actually incomplete since there are things it does not contain. For example, just as a starter, there is nothing specific about drysuit valves, seals, off-board dumps, mask, backup mask or fins!

Also missing from most checklists is a check to make sure the checks are carried out correctly. In aviation, military and other environments, checklists are worked through using the Challenge and Response method. One pilot reads each item to be checked from the checklist, while the second does the check and responds: a sort of "10-degrees of flap!" "10-degrees of flap, CHECK!" We do not see this happening in recreational diving. Perhaps we should. Checklists are not the

answer to everything, but they do shine a pretty bright light on a whole category of errors and potential failure points before anyone gets wet.

STEP TWO: Dive the Plan
The real fun part, and what makes everything else worth the effort, is the dive. The best advice I know is to dive as often as possible, enjoy, learn, and repeat frequently.

A CCR checklist carried on the back cover of the author's underwater notebook.

When I first started technical diving, I was surprised that one of my buddies was able to recount the dive blow-by-blow without missing a beat. I asked her how she managed to keep the whole of a 75-minute dive in sequence in her head without notes or any other kind of prompt. She introduced me to the concept of waypoints. Up until that time, even with several

hundred recreational dives scribbled into a logbook, not one person had mentioned waypoints, either as a mnemonic for remembering what happened on a dive or – more importantly – as a running check to reference the real-world experience against our blue-sky dive plan.

What I learned from my more creative buddy was that slicing dives up into bite-sized chucks rather than asking one's memory to swallow the dive as a whole, it was easier to remember what happened, to whom and when.

She filed both major and minor events on our dives in and around waypoints, like scribbled notes stuck under fridge magnets. If a huge seal suddenly appeared or someone dropped their backup light or it took longer than it should to get a buddy's attention, she slotted it into a virtual pigeon-hole between waypoints. She did a similar thing with gas volumes and was the first diver I had met who bothered to calculate, to the bar, what her SPG would read at various points during our dives together. This was handy to gauge how closely estimates of gas consumption (and by association, estimates of workload and stress) followed planned values long before any potential low-gas issues made themselves known.

In addition, having a set of basic waypoints, something one can use on just about every dive, helps to reinforce buddy communications and helps to prevent buddy separation especially among less experienced dive teams. Waypoints buttress the use of Go or Go Home buddy checks. The question asked at each waypoint is a simple: do we continue or is it time to bailout?

The default waypoints are:

1. Immediately before everyone either jumps into the water or just before everyone puts his or her head underwater for the dive to begin.

2. When the team conducts either the standard cave-style S-Drill (safety drill) or its modified version at a few metres depth. A safety drill is an exercise where each diver checks to make sure that the first stage they would donate to an out of air buddy in an emergency is not trapped under other kit, deploys easily and that both it and their backup regulator breathes properly. A modified S-drill includes an in-water, abbreviated version of the gear check conducted on dry land (such as making sure your buddy's drysuit inflator is connected, etc.), and a bubble check to make sure gas is not leaking from someplace that ought to be gas tight.

3. Arrival at target depth or, in the case of cave diving, at the transition from cavern to cave or where the "gold line" begins.

4. When the dive is turned (that's to say when the first team member reaches "team-thirds" or the pre-arranged "turn time" is reached).

5. Arriving back at the exit point or ascent line and preparing to ascend including making any decisions regarding on the schedule to follow to the surface.

6. The beginning of any required stops during ascent (including safety stops and staged decompression stops).

7. The final ascent to the surface is started.

8. Technically, a dive does not end until the surface interval is finished (up to 12 hours or more after the dive), but the last "waypoint" is making sure everyone feels fine when gear is stowed and the SIT begins.

These are the defaults, but there's absolutely nothing to stop you from adding your own, and of course, over-riding all these: the credo that any diver can call a dive at any time has precedence.

STEP THREE: Discuss the Plan

When I worked at a newspaper, part of my job was to write editorials: those little opinion pieces that comment on community happenings such as the mayor getting caught drunk driving, or a local kid winning a scholarship to Baliol College. After a few weeks on the job, the managing editor took me aside to explain that the purpose of an editorial was to point out the problem – the bit I was good at – but always and without fail to provide a workable suggestion on how to fix it – something my early attempts by-passed completely.

I listened and believe my editorials were more readable because I followed my more experienced colleague's advice. I'd give similar suggestions to those of you involved in dive debriefings. If you have something negative to say, fine, get it off your chest, but unless you know the solution, and have time to help explain and enact it, better to hold your piece until you do and can.

That said, a debriefing is designed to improve the diving experience next time around. If something was missing from an otherwise successful dive, it needs to be pointed out. If another member of the team did something totally unplanned and potentially or actually dangerous, that definitely needs to be discussed. There may not be a truly diplomatic way to bring a buddy's attention to weak skills or dangerous habits; but try your best. And if you don't have a perfect solution, at least ask! Perhaps another team member does.

If the issue is you, listen, don't try to defend an indefensible position, ask for help or suggestions how to fix things. Learn. A buddy with poor skills can be a liability, but one that realizes they need to work on one skill or another, is on their way to being an asset.

I no longer dive with a friend who simply refused to listen to ALL his former dive buddies. He had all the physical skills, but his mental ones were definitely suspect. His habit was to wander off during dives. On occasion – several occasions – he would simply disappear, which is not what anyone needs from a team member while cave diving. He is a smart and successful man and renowned in his field, but incapable of staying focused long enough to finish a dive as part of a team. If caves housed squirrels, he would surface with a cage full.

Of course, few dives turn out exactly as we imagined they would. Life tends to get in the way of dreams. Diving, especially a long technical dive, is dynamic and unexpected things happen... most of them interesting and enjoyable. Plans need to be organic and flexible enough to cover these types of events as well as the bad stuff. Work with an operations plan that fits your needs as closely as possible and that is strong enough to be modified and reused for future dives that may follow "the same" basic parameters.

For example, a dive on a wreck may present an opportunity to explore an area that's new and unknown. If your plan is flexible enough to allow you and your buddies to check it out, then do so. If that is not an option, stick to the original.

Aim for a dive plan and SOP that's a good fit, and during your post dive analysis, made adjustments to ensure an even better fit.

TWO AND A HALF SUGGESTED PROCEDURES... and something extra for sidemount divers

There is a real temptation in a book such as this, to cram it full of recommendations on how to do everything from selecting a mask that fits to a workable method to check for current-limited performance on a closed-circuit rebreather's bank of oxygen cells at 120 metres. As tempting as it may be, issues with space, time and common-sense eventually kick in and things have to be scaled back.

In the chapter on equipment – a single chapter that could easily have evolved into a 50,000-word stand-alone book on its own – focus was put on two pieces of equipment that are certainly 'techie' but whose use is growing more common among all types of recreational diving: a stage bottle and a delayed surface marker buoy (DSMB).

With that in mind, here are two and a half suggested procedures – drills essentially – that may help you to develop a good habit or best practice for your personal diving. The following is a suggested procedure taken from my personal SOP.

We'll start with the half procedure. This is not really much of a procedure, but more of a tip: a valuable one though. If you are in the habit of opening a scuba-tank valve and then partially closing it, please cut it out. It's a potentially dangerous practice based on some old-wives tale from a welding shop and has no place at any level of scuba diving.

It is standard practice in technical diving to dive with one's valves fully open or fully closed, no turning them partially off to "protect" the valve seat. First off, a modern valve seat really does not need protecting. Forcing it open may damage it but forcing it closed might too. If it's OK to close it fully, why isn't it OK to open it fully? In any event, a modern valve is pretty robust. Gentle opening and closing and an annual service will suffice to keep it working just fine. Secondly, on many occasions, an open and then partially closed valve has turned out to be a closed and then partially open valve. This is situation is very dangerous and remarkably common.

The problem is this: a partially open valve will deliver enough gas on the surface to go unnoticed (the SPG might flutter but it's unlikely the average diver will notice that because his regulator will breath normally). However, at depth, a valve in that state will not deliver enough gas and the diver will be starved of air.

This oversight has caused OOA panic in recreational divers resulting in death. One incident recently in Blue Springs, Florida resulted in a new diver dying with more than half a complete fill in his single tank. We can say that one trigger in this sad event was the silly, out-dated practice of "open valve fully and then close a quarter turn." This asinine piece of "diving lore" has caused countless panicked ascents, and innumerable complaints to rental departments that "The regs you gave me did not work at depth."

Make the switch now: gently open fully for diving: gently closed fully when finished. As long-time cave instructor and educator Harry Averill reminds his entry-level technical diving students when explaining this rule: "In the final analysis, the remote chance of valve damage beats the possibility of being dead."

DEPLOYING A STAGE BOTTLE REGULATOR

During any open-circuit staged decompression dive it is standard practice to switch from back gas to a more oxygen-rich gas at least once during ascent. Because of the potential risks associated with breathing high partial pressures of oxygen, divers are strongly advised to adopt a set procedure for gas switching which includes standardized safety protocols.

All scuba cylinders should be marked clearly according to standards agreed on by and adopted by the whole dive team. In addition, decompression cylinders should be marked with actual Maximum Operating Depth (MOD) of contents with removable tape on two sides of cylinder valve. This MOD must be based on recent analysis and calculations for acceptable dose of partial pressure at that marked MOD and should show NOTHING but MOD in meters or feet clearly marked in large numbers.

Decompression cylinders are usually worn on diver's left side with valve orifice facing diver and valve on/off knobs pointing to left. Divers enter water with regulator(s) on decompression cylinders charged and valve(s) closed.

During ascent, each diver will begin gas switch procedure prior to reaching switch depth (gas MOD). Deployment should follow the following steps.

Each team members "unstows" hose and second stage of selected decompression mix and pulls hose across her body with regulator second stage in right hand. Starting with dive leader, each members asks a buddy to "Look at my gas. Please confirm it is correct for next stop." Buddy must follow hose to first stage, read actual MOD and confirm that the regulator will deliver the correct gas for the coming gas switch. This query / confirmation cycle will be done one diver at a time.

Divers will then follow schedule and proceed to MOD for gas switch. Once there, they will switch regulators and with left hand on cylinder valve will breathe hose dry while checking SPG on selected decompression gas. As reading drops, indicating once again that regulator is indeed connected to the correct cylinder, they will carefully and slowly completely turn on the valve allowing decompression gas to flow normally. Once they are sure their regulator is breathing normally, they stow the back gas regulator they were formerly using. At the same time, each team member should indicate the status of their gas switch to dive leader. Once each team member has signaled "Switch went OK," elapsed time for decompression at that depth will start.

This procedure is repeated for each gas switch made during the dive.

Some further thoughts and notes: Do not breathe a gas which has not been analyzed by you or in your presence. There should be no exceptions to this rule. Secondly, it is imperative that all team members have similar decompression gases which can be switched within a depth of one meter or less.

Gas switching is perhaps the most stressful exercise performed during a normal ascent from a technical dive. It should never be executed in an off-hand or complacent way because the potential consequences of sloppy procedures are simply too severe. Second stage should be inspected for foreign matter -- muck, critters et al – before being breathed from.

Whenever possible, use decompression gases that all team members are familiar with such as EAN50, 50/25/25 and / or pure oxygen. However, when you are in the field and these "standard mixes" are NOT available, it is even more important (if that's possible) that you follow the procedure outlined here!

AND NOW FOR SOMETHING COMPLETELY DIFFERENT

A DSMB may be used in several ways and is a useful underwater tool; however, perhaps its most common use is as a signal marker to show surface support — such as a the captain and crew of one's charter boat – the dive team's position in the water during free and drifting ascents. It is this use that the following procedure will outline.

The following step-by-step procedure assumes use of marker buoy with an over-pressure valve connected to open-faced spool containing no less than 20 metres (70 feet) of #36 braided nylon knotted every 3 meters or ten feet.

A DSMB is a most effective way to signal a team's position in the water during an ascent away from a fixed ascent line in still water or during a drifting deco. The sealed or semi-sealed bags are preferred to an open-ended bag since open bags can deflate on the surface in moderately rough seas rendering them useless. All marker buoys should be brightly colored (but NOT white) and need to be marked to conform to any local regulations. In addition, it helps when diver's name is written somewhere near the bag's top with Sharpie-type black indelible felt-tipped pen.

Team deployment: single marker

Unless you are doing a skills session as part of an in-water assessment in a class, it's usual to deploy only one marker per dive team. This is often done when the team has reached relatively shallow water; sometime immediately prior to or following any gas switch at 21 metres (70-feet) for example.

The dive leader signals 'Deploy Marker' and team members confirm. Each member should carry a marker and a spool but part of the dive briefing will have covered off whose marker and spool is to be deployed. This team member will remove the spool and marker from her pocket or pouch, and display it for team to see. If the spool and marker are not pre-attached, she will do so and then hand the spool to her dive buddy. He will confirm that the line from the spool is firmly attached but ready to let out line unhindered and giving his buddy the "OK" signal, will continue to hold on to the spool. She will confirm this signal. After a final check to see that the line is not fouling any equipment, she will begin to inflate the marker (see below for suggested methods). When it has sufficient gas to rise towards the surface she will hold it away from her body and in the center of the buddy circle, Her team members will give the "OK" signal and she will then release the DSMB. The spool may be held lightly with the fingers or may be left to unroll itself freely in the water column with a cupped hand beneath it. When the marker reaches the surface, the line is tightened and re-clipped to prevent the spool from dropping into the depths.

The spool may be left in the center of the buddy circle providing a good visual reference. The spool's owner is usually responsible for rewinding line as the team continues its ascent, although this task can be shared. At no point is a spool or reel attached to any surface marker buoy to be clipped or tied to a diver.

Team deployment: multiple markers

Putting more than one bag and line up usually means the exercise is part of a skills session. In this case, deployment is done individually (see procedure below). However, each diver waits her turn to deploy her bag. Do not try to throw several bags (DSMBs) to the surface at once. You'll simply end up with a bird's nest of tangled lines.

Individual deployment

Take spool and marker from pocket ensuring that line is firmly attached to the marker. Hold spool in right hand and marker in left and show to buddy. They should confirm they have visually checked that you are clear to inflate. Begin to inflate marker until it is pulling lightly for the surface. Hold line and marker in front of you making sure no equipment is fouling the line. Watch for your buddy to give the OK signal and allow the marker to ascend.

Further notes:

A common mistake is over inflating a marker buoy so that it is impossible to control at depth. If a marker buoy starts to drag you up towards the surface, remember Boyle's Law: let it go immediately. The second most common mistake is under inflating it! To be effective, a DSMB must float upright with at least its top half out of the water.

A compact DSMB with a Schrader valve type inflation system and over-pressure safety valve. This model has a sealed bottom.

This requires it to be filled with gas and for the diver below to put some downward force on the line. This will help keep the inflated buoy visible to surface support personnel.

There are several ways to fill a DSMB. Semi-closed models can be filled by transferring gas from the wing into the bag using the LP (low-pressure) inflator/deflator. Additional gas can be added to the bag using the wing inflator but be careful to add gas in short spurts especially in cold water. Closed bags are inflated with an LP inflation hose. This can be a dedicated hose attached to a stage bottle or the drysuit hose can be disconnected from the suit, used to inflate the bag and then can be reconnected.

Exhaling into a bag may work but it puts the bag and the line attached to it very close to the diver's face and gear. Entanglement is a real possibility. Purging a spare regulator into a bag may work in warm water but can be a guaranteed way to start a freeflow in colder climates.

Divers should practice DSMB deployment in shallow water when they have no decompression or safety stop obligation.

It's vital that divers break surface no more than three meters from the marker especially where surface traffic or heavy seas may be a factor.

Diver alert markers can also be used to signal surface support that there is a problem with the dive team. Some advocate the use of different colored bags for this. I am not entirely comfortable with that option. I prefer instead the practice of sending a second marker up the same line. A message slate or note can be attached to the first or second bag explaining the problem. Naturally, whichever practice you opt to use, it is necessary to discuss this with your surface support prior to EVERY dive.

ONE LAST TIP ABOUT DSMB and SPOOL
Knotting the line on a spool (say every three metres or ten feet) can help you measure things like the length of a hatch cover or how far you are from the surface Very handy and reassuring in low-vis situations, and required when you practice bag deployment with mask off or blacked out.

REGULATOR SWITCHING FOR SIDEMOUNT DIVING: a suggestion
Sidemount diving seems like the new and trendy way to dive doubles, which is fine and I'm comfortable with that. But what's not so comforting is that depending on who trained them – or if they had training at all – many new sidemount divers seem confused about when and how to switch regulators. Since they are diving independent cylinders, this switching is one major new "skill" that divers have to learn.

The procedure that's presented here is what I do and teach. It works for most applications. It's a method shared by a bunch of other sidemount instructors and divers. You may find it works for you.

I wrote about it originally for X-Ray Magazine (perhaps the most exceptional onLine diving magazines), and I think the folks there for allowing me to reproduce the graphic they created to help illustrate the steps the method involves.

I started my magazine article explaining that of all the reasons that there may be to switch to sidemount for overhead diving, safety is number one in my opinion. I went on to explain what I meant.

"The basic aspects of gas management are essentially no different regardless of whether a diver is wearing a set of twins or carrying sidemount. But there are a couple of other "skills" that make me believe that a sidemount configuration is safer than traditional backmount. And these are the skills used when preserving gas volume in the event of kit failure.

In the simplest possible terms, this boils down to the position of the cylinder valves, hand wheels, and regulator first stages, and the various hoses supplying gas. There are where the diver can see them. There is nothing important behind the diver's head. The major components of her life-support system are right where she can see them, identify the issue and react to it appropriately in the timeliest fashion possible. Having spent around 20 years teaching people how and watching them execute valve shutdowns while wearing traditional back-mounted twins, there is no doubt in my mind which is easier to manage... which is safer.

There are arguments made about the perceived advantages of a modern isolation manifold when things go pear-shaped: most commonly that with a tank valve turned off, the gas in the effected cylinder is still available to the diver.

No question, that is correct. However, when the correct protocols are followed, in the event of an incident that requires the diver to bailout and shut off a tank, the dive is over, finished, done and dusted. And when the correct gas volume protocols are followed, the volume of gas available to a sidemount diver with one side compromised, is more than sufficient to get them out of the water.

I guess, I should explain something about gas switching too. Actually, I believe the fact that a SM diver switches second stages during her dive is another advantage that SM has over traditional back mount breathing the long hose. There's probably a whole 1000 words on the potential scenarios where this would show itself, but the short form is that our SM diver knows both her second stages are working... she always knows.

The argument made by stuck-fast doubles divers that breathing the longhose and having it ready to donate it in the event of an emergency OOA situation, it largely spurious.

Firstly, ask an experienced technical diver how many emergency OOA situations he or she has experienced when diving with advanced or technical divers? When gas management guidelines are followed, these situations are rare: extremely rare.

(If you are diving with classically trained OW divers who have been taught to believe that gas volume management includes a Controlled Emergency Swimming Ascent as a viable option, your mileage may vary but a straw poll of all the folks in the head office of TDI in Maine a few years ago turned up just how rare this type of situation is. Between us we had in excess of 14,000 dives on doubles and in SM, and we could only cite one example of an emergency OOA and that was an open-water diver who had followed a group into an overhead unnoticed.)

Anyhow, let's get back to that protocol for switching between regulators and how well this technique helps to preserve a nice cushion of spare gas for a buddy in the event that something DOES go wrong.

There are several methods but the one I use and teach to folks who are team diving is this. It requires only THREE regulator switches for the whole dive... well at least until the decompression gas is reached.

The dive starts by breathing from the right-hand cylinder (the bottle at the diver's right side... which is usually fitted with a long hose), and ends with the diver breathing from the bottle at her left side.

OK. Take as given that the diver has worked out her gas volumes and knows how many bar represent thirds and how many bar represent one half of one of those thirds. To make this somewhat clearer, let's say that one third of our diver's available pressure is 60 bar, therefore, one sixth is 30 bar.

She begins her dive and breathes from her right cylinder until its pressure has dropped by 30 bar, and then she switches to her left cylinder.

She breathes from it until the pressure drops by 60 bar, and she switches back to her right tank. For the record, her left cylinder is now at thirds.

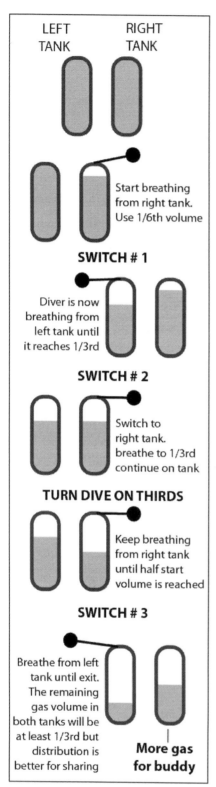

LEFT TANK   RIGHT TANK

Start breathing from right tank. Use 1/6th volume

SWITCH # 1

Diver is now breathing from left tank until it reaches 1/3rd

SWITCH # 2

Switch to right tank. breathe to 1/3rd continue on tank

TURN DIVE ON THIRDS

Keep breathing from right tank until half start volume is reached

SWITCH # 3

Breathe from left tank until exit. The remaining gas volume in both tanks will be at least 1/3rd but distribution is better for sharing

More gas for buddy

She breathes her right tank until its pressure has dropped by 30 bar and at this point, she is at thirds in both tanks and signals to her buddies to turn the dive... However, she continues to breath from that right-hand bottle until its pressure has dropped a further 30 bar. She is about to switch for the third and last time... but let's just recap a couple of things. The bottle at her left side has two-thirds its starting pressure (plus a small reserve if she is in an overhead). The one on her right that she has just finished breathing from, contains one half of its starting pressure (one-sixth plus one third is three sixths, which equals a half).

OK, so our diver has switched for the last time and is breathing gas from her left cylinder and she and her buddies are on their way home. The tank she is breathing from has sufficient gas to get her there.

She will at the end of the dive, should everything go according to Hoyle have at least one third of her starting volume preserved in her tanks. The only difference is that more of that contingency gas is contained in the cylinder to her right... the one with a long hose... the one she would share with her buddy if something hit the fan.

There are a bunch of reasons to dive SM, but for me, especially in a virtual or real overhead environment, the most important one is that from the perspective of gas management, I believe it is the safest option.

WHEN THINGS GO SIDEWAYS: A low-fibre version of Fault Tree Analysis

Occasionally – and I hope for you extremely rarely or never – a dive goes completely off-kilter. We exit the water wondering what caused things to go so far sideways in such a short space of time, and perhaps only to ourselves, admit we're lucky Muppets who should be glad that we are still standing up.

You may never experience this type of event or the epiphany that follows. But, just in case someone asks, the best reaction is to take it as a serious opportunity to learn something about human nature and the vagaries of diving that's more valuable than anything to be found in a textbook.

We have any number of ways to work out what caused things to go wrong and how to prevent or sidestep those things next time. You and I have spent the past several chapters looking at "tools" to help us in this regard. But let's introduce a couple of different ways to analyse things that go pear-shaped. You may find one or both useful concepts: or you may find both too complex and overblown and have an alternative. It really does not matter which method you prefer to use. What does matter is that you have some way to deconstruct a "special" surprise and learn from it.

I introduce students just beginning their technical diver training to a very basic form of Fault Tree Analysis, and a less structured but equally effective logic tree analysis based on similar principles.

Fault tree analysis (FTA) is a process designers and engineers (and project managers) use to identify problems with existing products and services. It is part of a structured quality planning / quality assurance process, and FTA is also used to improve products and services by examining critical features and designing around human error. FTA highlights what causes trouble and what remedies and countermeasures can overcome that trouble.

A full-blown fault tree diagram uses different shaped objects to represent major faults or critical failures associated with a product or service, what causes faults in the system, and potential fixes. The analyst selects a component for analysis, identifies critical

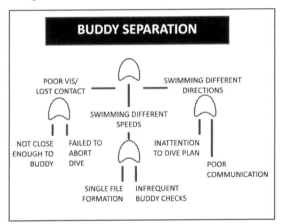

failures or "faults" related to the component then lists applicable causes for those faults until what's called a root cause is identified. Then countermeasures or corrective actions are attached to these root causes, by other graphic elements.

The figure above shows an extremely simple fault tree diagram.

The issue being analyzed with it is buddy separation. For this example, we have listed the problems as: lost visual contact; divers swimming at different speeds; and divers swimming in different directions as most common. Each of these causes is a "stand-alone" in this diagram and is connected with the fault (buddy

separation) by the graphic element that signifies an OR statement.

For each of the three causes of buddy separation, the diagram lists a couple of contributing causes or effects. For lost visual contact it highlights the dive team failing to keep close or not thumbing the dive as soon as it was apparent that the vis was awful.

Contributing factors to the cause swimming at different speeds, are shown as divers swimming in a single file formation, and divers conducting buddy checks too infrequently. This would be particularly true of the diver in the lead, wouldn't it? When divers swim in different directions, the diagram indicates that the team has ignored their dive plan, or have poor communications skills.

A "Cheap and Cheerful" analysis of the problem of buddy separation as described in our fault tree diagram might go something like this.

1.   To help lessen the risk of buddy or team separation, members should be mindful of losing contact because of poor visibility. If divers find the visibility poor during the dive, they should 1/ maintain close visual contact OR if visual contact is compromised 2/ abort the dive.

2.   At all times, the team must swim at the same rate otherwise separation becomes more likely. Having the team swim side-by-side and conduct frequent buddy checks is the best strategy, but if swimming in single file is necessary, buddy checks must be made more frequently than usual.

One other issue is when a member of the team swims off in a different direction to his buddy(ies). A strong dive plan will only minimize this risk if it is followed at all times. Any mild deviation from this plan (for example, swimming "off track" to explore something that looks interesting), should only be made if all team members can agree on the change, which requires excellent communications (signs/notebook/slate).

You can buy FTA software with which you can build complex diagrams and analyse hugely intricate systems using Boolean operators and every one of a dozen or so fault tree diagram shapes: if you wish.

A cheaper alternative is to use a simple logic tree based on similar principles, identifying top-level events, faults, causes, root causes, and countermeasures. All you need is a spreadsheet program or a table created in your favorite word processing application.

The chart overleaf shows an example of fault analysis used with students who are learning about technical diving. It lists some of the issues that might occur, the causes and appropriate countermeasures.

Although an incomplete listing, it presents a worthwhile exercise in the contingency planning process. The problem is loss of deco gas from a 6 litre - 40 c/ft aluminum bottle.

CATASTROPHIC GAS LOSS FROM SMALL VOLUME CYLINDER CONTAINING DECOMPRESSION GAS			
FAULT	**CAUSE**	**ROOT CAUSE**	**COUNTERMEASURE**
Burst disc failure (Rupture disk failure)	Extremely high-pressure	Filling beyond rated pressure; storage of filled tank in high heat	Fill tanks to less than rated rupture pressure; store correctly
	Not high-pressure	Age or mechanical damage	Replace at least annually
Extruded neck o-ring	Extremely high-pressure	Filling beyond rated pressure; storage of filled tank in high heat	Fill tanks to less than rated rupture pressure; store correctly
	Not high-pressure	Dislodged mechanically	Store correctly during transportation
HP/LP hose bleeding gas	Leak from crimp	Faulty manufacture	Replace (warranty)
	Cracked hose casing	Age; distorting or bending hose	Replace
	Leak from o-ring	Incorrect assembly; broken o-ring	Replace with new o-ring, do not over tighten during assembly
Free-flowing regulator	Second stage malfunction	Venturi effect; frozen first stage	Turn off, wait, disengage venture (if fitted), try again; feather valve
	First stage malfunction	Incorrect IP; HP seat problem; cold operation; over-breathing	Turn off, wait, try again; feather valve. Inspect and adjust on surface

LEADERSHIP: A suggested plan for staying real and managing risk

One of the most interesting dynamics of technical diving – both during planning and execution – revolves around the issue of leadership. It's not simply a question of who leads and who follows but a much more complex balancing act between responsibilities, experience, team composition and dive goals.

Since technical diving is recognized as a high-risk, team-oriented activity, coming up with the correct answers can mean the difference between a great dive and a bad experience.

I guess the most important first step is to understand what we mean by leadership and the factors that inform that definition.

We should start by pointing out that one of the fundamental guidelines recommended is: "The weakest diver leads the dive."

Now weakest in this context is not an assessment of physical strength or mental fortitude – although these may be factors in some cases. More usually a diver may be "weak" because he or she has less experience with the particular sort of dive being planned and how best to achieve the dive's specific goals; or they may start the dive with another more subtle disadvantage. On some ocean dives, weakest may be the diver most prone to seasickness and who has taken meds to help deal with that particular stress. It may also be the diver who among his or her peers on the particular day in question wakes up the least rested or most stressed... as in "I'll lead the dive today because I had a restless night."

Whatever the actual reason for "weakness" the logic behind this guideline is that it helps eliminate "trust me dives." In cases where the least experienced diver is the leader, it also offers the best opportunity for that diver to expand his or her comfort zone. Let's take the example of a cave dive with a three-person team. For this example, let's say that two of the team have explored the cave on several occasions but for one, this is her first time in.

All three may be experienced cave divers, but one is certainly at a slight disadvantage. By having her take charge of the dive, two things are assured. Firstly, she will not be directed by a more self-assured buddy into a situation which she finds uncomfortable. Her level of comfort on the dive will most likely be increased since it will go at her pace, and with two companions to "guide" her when the time comes to make a decision – for example "is this the right side-passage to take..." – her comfort zone may be expanded but not breached.

The result will most likely be a much more enjoyable dive for everyone involved since stress levels can be better managed.

This example of leadership during the actual execution of a cave dive may not relate directly to the type of diving you do, but the logic is transferable to all varieties of technical or complex advanced diving whether in a hard overhead environment or not.

It also introduces us to some of the complexities that surrounds the various roles that team members take on in technical diving, and the interrelationship of leadership, coaching, mentorship and mutual support in the process of learning.

Let's recap and redefine a little. The weakest diver leads during the EXECUTION of a dive, but this diver would most likely take a backseat role during the actual PLANNING of that same dive.

If we go back to our example, let's travel by time-machine to a day or two before the execution of the dive to the time our three dive buddies sat down together to plan the dive. We know that all three are experienced cave dives and during their initial assessment of the dive's parameters they agreed that each had the appropriate training, familiarity with the required equipment, and general experience in the type of environment. What was apparent was that one needed a detailed briefing on the specifics on the dive since she had never been to the site before. This is where the dynamics of "team diving" come into play.

In old-school terms, leadership might be interpreted as the behavior of a tartar or martinet. A person who demands strict adherence to his or her rules and any deviation from those rules will result in some sort of punitive reaction: verbal or otherwise. I am reasonably sure that many of you have first-hand experience of this form of bullying and "management" by intimidation. There is no place for this style of bullying in technical diving… or anywhere else actually. It may have worked to send hapless souls over the trenches during WWI but is about as useful in diving as ashtrays on a motorcycle. There is simply no room for this attitude anywhere close to technical divers planning their dive.

The leader during this stage needs to be empathetic, supportive and their role is more akin to a coach or mentor: someone who encourages others to contribute ideas and suggestions. A real leader shares knowledge, has real information, suggests better alternatives when asked, and gets satisfaction from helping others grow. Essentially, a good leader produces good leaders.

In the example of the planning for the cave dive, the leader might respond to questions about distances and times with something like: "what do you feel comfortable doing?" rather than pushing his or her agenda. In fact, an important part of the mentoring process is to promote the goals of others even when it makes their own subordinate.

For most of dives, up-front considerations of leadership are a little over-the-top. The vast majority of dives – even technical ones – follow a pattern that is established within the team and roles and responsibilities are simple, understood and virtually unspoken. Often on this type of dive, leadership amounts to little more than: "Hey Jill, how about you run the reel today?" But when game-day brings those special dives… the apex dives for your team… give special consideration to the dynamics of team leadership. Oh, and remember that changing circumstances at depth, may alter who is "weakest" and may require change of "leadership!"

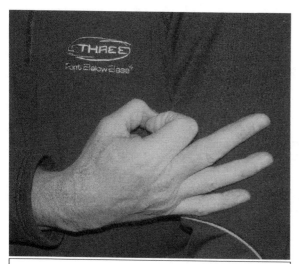

A useful hand signal when team leadership needs to be switched from one diver to another. Three fingers slapped on the arm or shoulder signifying "rank" followed by pointing at the diver to whom leadership has been switched.

Never be reluctant to "take the lead" and call a dive, and remember that whoever thumbed a dive in those circumstances, automatically is now the one who calls the shots. They may very well need a helping hand, but it's their call who does what, when, how and to whom until everyone is safely back on the surface.

A hand signal that you will not find in any book but that over the years my friends and I have found useful and effective: it signifies: "You take control: you lead!"

Get you buddy's or the team's attention, and make the OK signal with either hand. Then bring that hand and the OK signal down, slap the three fingers "left over" against the opposite forearm or bicep (think of your fingers as a sergeant's stripes) then point to the person who is taking over leadership.

IN CLOSING

Perception of risk changes over time. The more successful we are at beating the odds, the less risky we take our behavior to be; and of course, the opposite may be true. Too often, luck reinforces bad decisions and dilutes fear, and fear is surely part of the apparatus, our personal filter, for risk management. We each must understand that because someone surfaces from a dive with a smile on their face, it does not mean they follow a good risk management process or that their behavior is not risky. It is impossible to measure a negative. Vigilance is required.

I am sitting in my office wrapping up this project. There is snow on the ground outside and I will soon have to pack and get ready to fly to Europe and go to yet another interesting and very big dive show. Perhaps I should feel happy, but I do not: I am sad.

Yesterday evening I got news that a father and son (a boy of 15 who had earned no level of scuba certification at all) had both drowned in the Eagles Nest Cave, an advanced-level North Florida system considered a challenge to certified and experienced trimix cave divers. They were, according to family, testing out new gear the kid had been given for Christmas. What on earth were they thinking: what was the father thinking as he died? The previous week, two more technical divers perished. One in the Red Sea and one in the caves of Mexico. I knew them both. One much better than the other but both were nice guys; both were experienced, and unlike the father/son combination who died in a spot where neither belonged, both of last week's victims were what one would call careful divers.

Fatal dive accidents frequently have multiple and complex, often interconnected, root causes. While each accident has unique qualities about it – in part because of the individuals involved – most accidents can be characterized as a chain of small events that lead to disaster.

This chain of events very often starts with a minor challenge – a failure in communications, a broken strap – and one event meshes with a deficiency or mistake elsewhere and triggers something even more serious, and this in turn results in escalating calamities until the house of cards has fallen down completely. To stay on top of things, technical divers need to become pretty slick at recognizing problems early, preventing a chain reaction, and thereby avoiding a one-way ride to calamity. Often something as simple as calling a dive early, before anyone gets close to the edge, can change the outcome radically and turn a potentially nasty epiphany into a positive learning experience.

Gareth Lock, who was kind enough to write the foreword for this book, is a Royal Air Force officer with a background in risk analysis and management. In his writings and presentations, he shares with us a refreshingly analytical view of dive accidents.

He and I arrive at a similar destination via quite different analytical pathways. Based on his background in the military, he uses what he calls the **HFACS Dive Model** (pronounced H – FACS-D). His analysis and methods are based on the Human Factors Analysis and Classification System framework developed by Dr. Douglas Wiegmann and Dr. Scott Shappell of the United States Navy to identify why accidents happen and how to reduce their impact and frequency. Gareth suggests that for a dive accident to occur, several contributing factors have to align. These factors may include organizational influence, unsafe supervision, a pre-condition for unsafe acts, and unsafe acts themselves.

I believe the factors, the triggers, that lead to deaths like the recent ones in a Florida cave, the Red Sea, and Mexico are more personal, more within our grasp. The survival techniques identified back in the 1990s: Attitude, Knowledge, Training, Gas Supply, Gas Toxicity, Exposure, Equipment and Operations, provide divers with a laundry list of potential dangers.

Gareth points out with some clarity, that people 'get away' with diving 'successfully' when there are errors at every level in his HFACS model: they simply did not align that day. "And that," he tells us. "Reinforces bad decisions and creates diver complacency."

One has to agree with him regardless of how or why you feel divers are dying so frequently. It seems to me that ignoring just one of the eight suggested survival techniques may be enough to begin a series of events that end in death: it may take two or three, and a lucky diver may get away with ignoring four or five without an incident. Life is not fair that way.

Finally, Gareth reminds us: "It is easy to blame a person, when the system is actually at fault."

I believe too that we are sometimes too quick to blame the individual and often do not trace the mistakes made back to their "systemic" roots. But sometimes all or the majority of fault does rest with a single person. The system did its best and the best is all we can expect of anything outside of demanding a nanny state. In some instances, the buck comes to a full stop hard against the victim's attitude, their ignorance, their lack of training, their history of flaunting the rules, their willingness to gamble with the odds.

Every day you and I, indeed the whole diving community, are faced with a dilemma: whether to commit an error of omission or an error of commission. In cases where we know someone is pushing their luck, do we mind our own business, remain quiet and watch as they hurt themselves or their dive buddies; or do we speak out? If we do consider ourselves part of a system that Gareth and others say needs fixing, do we have the tools to carry out the repairs? Do we even know what to fix and where to start? Can we make a difference?

There's a kid throwing starfish back into the sea as the tide recedes. A guy walks up and asks him what he's up to. "Saving lives," he explains. "The tide is going out and these starfish will die on the beach, so I'm throwing them back in." The man laughs and tells the kid that the beach is miles long and that there are hundreds, probably thousands of stranded starfish. He tells the kid he can't save them all. The kid stops what he's doing, looks at the guy, looks up at the sky, and back out at the ocean. He bends down, picks up another starfish and throws it as far out to sea as he can. "Saved that one!"

My hope is that through all this effort, I may just get one person to think twice before starting a dive with a faulty oxygen cell, or breathing a gas that hasn't been analyzed, or dismissing a buddy's suggestion that today is not a good day to go diving, or taking an unqualified diver to a trimix-depth cave to test new gear. Help me save a starfish.

GLOSSARY

A

Absolute Pressure/Ambient Pressure: Total static pressure at the reference point. Pressure relative to a vacuum. Pressure at depth that takes into account atmospheric and hydrostatic pressure.

ADV, Automatic Diluent Valve: A demand valve set into the breathing loop of a rebreather to inject diluent gas into the loop when the loop volume drops and there is not enough gas for inhalation.

Alternative Air Source: A secondary supply of air or other breathing gas used by the diver in an emergency

Ambient Pressure Diving, APD: U.K. based company manufacturing several scuba products including the Inspiration, Evolution and Evolution+ family of rebreathers all using its proprietary Vision Software.

ANSTI: Ansti Test Systems Ltd is a U.K. company specializing in the design and manufacture of test facilities for performance measurement of underwater breathing apparatus. Considered by many to be the gold-standard in third-party testing for the scuba industry.

ATA: A deprecated unit of pressure used in few applications outside of diving. One ata or "atmosphere" (atm), is equal to 1.01325 bar. For brevity, the terms ATA and BAR are used interchangeably in most diving textbooks including this one.

B

Back Gas: Breathing gas carried by a scuba diver in back mounted cylinders. Generally the primary breathing gas for the bottom or deepest sector of a dive.

Backplate: A plate, normally made from metal, which rests against the diver's back, and to which the primary scuba cylinders are attached. Held to the body by harness straps over the shoulders and round the waist. Sometimes also crotch straps and chest straps. Usually used with a back inflation buoyancy compensator.

Back Mount: The practice of carrying scuba tank or tanks on the diver's back, supported by a harness, backplate or Buoyancy Control Device (BCD).

BAR: The bar is a unit of pressure defined using the SI unit pascal, and one bar is equal to: 100 kPa or roughly normal atmospheric air pressure at sea level. One bar = 14.5 psi.

Bird's Nest, Birds Nested: The name given to a reel or spool on which the line has become extremely tangled and difficult to correct while underwater.

Boolean Operator: A mathematical construct that gives a simple yes/no, on/off, black/white choice.

BSAC: British Sub-Aqua Club, is the UK's leading dive club and the sport's National Governing Body, providing an internationally-recognised diver training and development programme via a network of clubs and centres across the country and overseas.

Bubble Check: Part of a proper team/buddy check carried out at the start of a dive before committing to depth or penetration. Consists of visual check of buddy's gear looking for gas leaks: bubbles.

Bubble Model: A class of decompression algorithms. Bubble models, and similar adaptations of Neo-Haldanian algorithms that include deep stop profiles, have become the standard for technical and deep diving, with many training agencies including bubble models into their courses.

Bungee Loop (old-school or Armadillo): Loop of strong elastic cord designed to loop over a tank valve's hand wheel and pull the tank in close against the diver's side.

C

CCR, Closed-Circuit Rebreather: An under-water life-support system that recycles exhaled gas, scrubs it of carbon-dioxide and recirculates it back to the diver. Pre-dates open-circuit scuba gear.

CESA: Controlled Emergency Swimming Ascent. A technique taught to beginning sport divers as a means of getting themselves to the surface when faced with an out of air situation. Absolutely a last resort option because many deaths and serious injuries have been sustained by divers attempting CESA in real emergencies.

Chillicothe Baking Company: American bakery attributed with selling the first loaves of sliced bread.

Coles Notes: Series of books published to help high-school students produce homework such as book reports without actually reading the book! A Canadian concept!

Controlling Volume: In a team of divers the diver who begins the dive with the least amount of gas (measured in litres or cubic feet) has the controlling volume and all gas calculations for the group are made using that figure.

D

Dalton's Law: States that the total pressure exerted by the mixture of non-reactive gases is equal to the sum of the partial pressures of individual gases. Named for chemist John Dalton and used by divers to calculate the quantity or dose of a specific gas (primarily oxygen, secondarily nitrogen) in a breathing mixture.

DCI: Is a blanket term covering two separate injuries: decompression sickness (DCS), caused by nitrogen bubbles that form in the bloodstream, and arterial gas embolism (AGE), caused by lung over-pressurization.

DCS: Short form for Decompression Sickness. DCS is a complex collection of maladies resulting from a change or sudden decrease in pressure during underwater ascent, usually occurring during free or assisted dives but also a threat in high-altitude aviation.

Decompression, Deco: The process of slowly ascending from a dive to facilitate the elimination of gases accumulated in during the course of a dive and to lessen the risk of decompression sickness. Although it is said that all dives are deco dives, a decompression dive usually involves one or several staged stops of several minutes each before the diver can surface.

Diluent, Dil: Breathing gas carried as part of CCR (usually on the diver's left side) and used to dilute oxygen (usually carried on the right) so that the gas in the loop of a closed circuit rebreather delivers an oxygen partial pressure suited to the depth.

DIN: Deutsches Institut für Normung (German Institute for Standardization), or 'DIN' is the official national-standards body, representing German interests at the international and European levels. In diving DIN is used to describe the type of fitting on a regulator first stage that screws into a corresponding DIN tank valve. Available in 300 bar and 200 bar versions.

DSMB: Delayed Surface Marker Buoy is deployed from depth generally near the end of a dive to mark the diver's position underwater during a safety stop or staged decompression stops so that members of surface support team (a boat crew for instance) can easily locate them. A reel or spool and line connect the buoy on the surface to the diver beneath the surface.

Doing What Works/DW²: A semi-serious suggestion by American cave explorer Larry Green as a tag to be used as an alternative to the various cave and technical diving "philosophies" being touted as "Hogarthian" between the late 1990s and the first few years of the 21st century. Green, among many other industry observers, felt that the Hogarthian method had been distorted and diluted so much, and was being applied to such widely divergent ways of diving (both safe and unsafe) that the term Hogarthian had become meaningless. The term is in general use in fields as different as medicine, education and politics.

E

EANx: Nitrox, and short form for Enriched Air Nitrox with the x sometimes replaced with the percentage of oxygen in the mix; as in EAN32 for a 32 percent oxygen mix.

END: Equivalent Nitrogen Depth or Equivalent Narcotic Depth. The depth at which the narcotic effects of nitrogen in a given breathing mixture at a given depth is approximately equivalent to the effects of air. Sometimes used to designate the nitrogen depth of a trimix breathing gas and its suitability for a dive to a specific depth (e.g. "Our mix will give us an END of 27 metres at our target depth of 67 metres.)

Exley, Sheck: American cave-diving pioneer born, April 1, 1949, died, April 6, 1994. Exley is credited with several innovative ideas intended to improve diver safety including helping to standardize the usage of the "octopus," a redundant second stage regulator. He wrote several articles and two books: *Caverns Measureless to Man*, and *Basic*

Cave Diving: A Blueprint for Survival. He worked as a mathematics teacher in a North Florida High School. Died trying to reach the bottom of a cenote in Mexico more than 300 metres deep.

F

Feathering, Feather Breathing: Technique for emergency breathing from a freeflowing demand regulator where the diver manually controls air flow by opening and closing the cylinder valve.

Fuel Cell: An electro-galvanic fuel cell is the electrical device used to measure the partial pressure of oxygen gas in scuba diving and medical equipment. The output from fuel cells is susceptible to fluctuations caused by moisture, temperature and age. They have a limited shelf-life. **(See also Oxygen Cell.)**

Freeflow: Malfunction of a scuba regulator when the valve sticks in the open position, allowing a constant rate of gas to flow.

Frog Kick: Swimming technique where thrust is developed by sweeping the fins horizontally toward each other with the fins twisted into a nearly vertical plane, with the soles facing each other.

G

Gay-Lussac's Law: Chemical law describing the relation between temperature and pressure in an ideal gas for a constant volume.

Gauge Mode: Switching the operating mode of a PDC (personal dive computer) so decompression calculations are disabled and the unit operates as a timer and depth gauge. Typically used when a team of divers opt to use proprietary decompression tables and/or members of a dive team have PDCs using vastly differing algorithms.

Gilliam, Bret: Underwater photographer, author, publisher. Founder of TDI and instrumental in popularizing deep, trimix diving in recreational market.

Gold Line: The permanent guideline left in the main thoroughfare of a cave system. Usually yellow or gold 3mm braided line with its starting point usually well inside the cave at the end of the cavern area.

Goodman Handle: A hard (metal) or soft (cloth) handle used to carry the primary dive light head comprising a slot through which the fingers and palm of the hand are extended, so that the light rests on the back of the hand, facing the direction of the extended fingers.

H

Haldanian: Decompression models based on the principles described by Scotsman John Scott Haldane in the early 1900s.

Heliair: Blend of trimix made by adding air to helium. In open-circuit diving heliair is uncommon because the possible blends have in common a low ratio of oxygen to helium resulting in longer decompression times. In CCR diving, a common heliair diluent is 10/50, blended by topping a cylinder up with air when previously filled to half its working pressure with pure helium.

Helicopter Turn: Swimming (finning) manoeuver in which the diver uses small fin movements to rotate on the spot on a vertical axis while holding horizontal trim.

Helitrox: A trimix breathing gas containing more than 21 percent oxygen and a maximum 20 percent helium. A name made up by a certifying agency's marketing department.

Helium: A Noble Gas used in diving to dilute oxygen and nitrogen in a diver's breathing mix, thereby aiding in the control of narcosis and oxygen toxicity. Extremely light gas with a mass of approximately 4 grams per mole compared to oxygen's 32 grams per mole, nitrogen's 28 and argon's 40.

Heliox: Blend of helium and oxygen for narcosis-free scuba diving.

Henry's Gas Law: Chemical law that describes the relationship between the solubility of a given gas in a given liquid as pressure varies.

Hogarthian: Relating to or describing the Alpinist approach to gear selection, configuration and deployment attributed to William (Bill) Hogarth Main, a North Florida cave diving pioneer. A back plate, wing, doubles with manifold, primary second stage on a long hose connected to right post (right-hand valve on diver's manifold), with a back-up second stage on a bungee necklace and connected to the diver's left post is considered by many to be the founding tenets of Hogarthian gear configuration.

Hypercapnia: A dangerous potentially fatal state caused by an excessive level of carbon dioxide in the body.

Hyperoxic: A gas with excess oxygen content compared to air. In diving any gas delivering an oxygen partial pressure of more than 0.21 bar (any nitrox for example) is said to be hyperoxic.

Hypoxic: A gas with reduced oxygen content compared to air. In diving a gas delivering an oxygen partial pressure of less than 0.18 bar is said to be hypoxic.

I

IANTD: International Association of Nitrox and Technical Divers. One of the original training agencies focused on technical diver programs.

J

Jon Line: A short line used to connect a diver to an anchor line, allowing the diver to move a short distance away to decompress. Relieves crowding during latter stages of team decompression and facilitates holding position relative to an anchored boat in moderate to harsh current. A Jon line also helps compensate for vertical movement in the anchor line due to surface waves. Named after wreck-diver Jon Hulburt, who is credited with its invention.

Joule: the derived SI unit of work or energy; the work done when the point of application of a force of 1 newton is displaced through a distance of 1 metre in the direction of the force. One joule is equivalent to 1 watt-second.

K

K-Valve: Somewhat obscure term to describe a standard scuba cylinder valve without obsolete lever reserve mechanism found on old J-Valves.

L

Line Arrow: Triangular plastic line marker with two slots to attach it to thin line used in cave diving. Used to indicate the direction of the exit. Also called a Dorf Arrow.

M

Manifold, Isolation Manifold: Used to connect two diving cylinders so that gas will be drawn equally from both tanks during a dive. Associated with technical diving. Integral in the basic gas management strategy of Hogarthian diving. Its advantage is that the diver has two regulator first-stages at his disposal, and the design of the manifold allows access to the gas in both tanks in the event one regulator malfunctions and has to be shut down.

Metric System: Is an internationally agreed decimal system of measurement. The term is now often used as a synonym for "SI" the official system of measurement in almost every country in the world.

Millwall, Millwall Football Club: English professional football club now based in South Bermondsey, south-east London, and currently playing in the Football League Championship, the second tier of English football. Founded as Millwall Rovers in 1885, the team had home grounds situated in Isle of Dogs and New Cross before its move to nearby South Bermondsey in 1993. One of its supporters' chants at matches is "Nobody likes us... and we don't care."

Muppet: A family of puppets created by Jim Henson now a trademark of Disney subsidiary Muppets Studio LLC. The word's slang use describes a foolish, incompetent, easily-led person. Applied usually in a benign context.

N

NDL: No Decompression Limit is used to describe the parameters of a dive from which a direct ascent to the surface without stops is possible while the statistical probability of incurring DCS is slight. Used colloquially to define dives that are not deco dives.

Negative Pressure Test/Positive Pressure Test: Part of the bench-testing procedures to ensure a CCR unit is gas tight and not leaking.

Nitrox: A breathing mixture of oxygen and nitrogen (the two main constituents of atmospheric air) where the level of oxygen is more than 21 percent.

NOAA: National Oceanic and Atmospheric Administration. An agency associated with the US Department of Commerce charged with conservation, stewardship and science. Its mission is to understand

and predict changes in climate, weather, oceans, and coasts.

No Bubbles, No Bubbles Diving: Sport or technical diving activities conducted using a CCR.

Normoxic: A gas that delivers the same or very similar oxygen partial pressure as air: e.g. a 20/20 trimix would be considered Normoxic.

O

Octopus, Octo: a redundant regulator second stage that can be used as a backup in the event that the diver's primary second stage fails, or alternatively to allow the diver and his buddy to have simultaneous access to his gas if the buddy has an out-of-gas emergency.

Off-Gassing/Off-Gassing Ceiling: State where a diver is decompressing from a dive. A theoretical spot in a diver's ascent where there is more inert gas leaving his body than entering it.

OOA/Out of Air: A situation in which a diver has either exhausted his gas supply or an equipment malfunction prevents access to an otherwise available gas supply.

Open-Circuit, OC: Traditional scuba gear which allows a diver's exhaled breath to escape in the form of bubbles.

Oxygen Cell, Oxygen Sensor: Small device used to test oxygen partial pressures in scuba and medical equipment. It works because **a** chemical reaction occurs when the potassium hydroxide in the cell comes into contact with gases containing oxygen. This creates a small electric current between the lead anode and the gold-plated cathode through a load resistance. The current produced, measured in millivolts is proportional to the concentration (partial pressure) of oxygen present. (**See Fuel Cell.**)

P

PADI: The Professional Association of Diving Instructors is the world's largest recreational diver training organization founded in 1966 by John Cronin and Ralph Erickson. Originally formed to break diver training down into different courses instead of the single universal course then prevalent.

Partial Pressure: The hypothetical pressure of each individual gas in a mixture of gases if it alone occupied the volume of the mixture at the same temperature. In a gas mix with 30 percent oxygen content at normal atmospheric pressure, the oxygen partial pressure would be 0.30 bar. At two atmospheres the percentage of oxygen would be unchanged but its partial pressure would be doubled to 0.60 bar.

Pear-Shaped: Round or spherical is perfect, pear-shaped is abnormal, broken or busted. Used to describe any process or thing that has unexpectedly gone wrong.

Pneumothorax: Condition in which air or another breathing gas has managed to enter a diver's chest cavity, often resulting in a collapsed lung.

PSI: Pounds or pound-force per square inch is a unit of stress used to describe the internal pressure of gas in a high-pressure cylinder. Working pressures of 3000 psi are common in scuba tanks. Atmospheric pressure at sea level (standard): Pa = 14.7 psi.

Punter: English/Australian colloquial term for a paying guest or a customer. Also used to describe an amateur gambler, usually one betting on horse racing or casino card games.

Q

Quick Link: Small oval metal connector shaped like a chain link with a screw gate on one side.

R

Rebreather: Shortened form of semi-closed circuit or closed-circuit rebreather, often used to describe both or either.

Recreational Diving: Any dive activity done for fun (i.e. any scuba not for military, scientific, research, commercial, or public safety/law enforcement tasks). Both sport and technical diving fall into the recreational diving category.

Rubicon Foundation: Is a non-profit organization undertaking projects that: Contribute to the interdependent dynamic between research, exploration, science and education; Improve the available resources for students, professionals and the general public; and preserve the valuable natural resources that are vital to future endeavors. More information at http://www.rubicon-foundation.org

Rutkowski, Richard "Dick": The godfather of Nitrox diving. A highly regarded pioneer in many fields relating to diver safety. He worked at NOAA from 1970 until 1985 as Deputy Diving Coordinator, Director of the NOAA Miami Hyperbaric Facility and Director of NOAA Diver Training. Also the founder of American Nitrox Divers International (ANDI), the International Association of Nitrox and Technical Divers (IANTD), and the Undersea Research Foundation (URF).

S

Scrubber, Carbon-Dioxide Scrubber: Component of a rebreather housing the material used to remove carbon dioxide from the diver's exhaled breath. Informally used to describe the **Soda lime** itself.

Semi-Closed Circuit Rebreather, SCR: Also called a gas extender. A life-support system which recycles most of diver's exhaled gas using similar technology to a full CCR but bleeds a small percentage out into the environment.

SI, SI UNIT: International System of Units is the modern form of the metric system and is the world's most widely used system of measurement, used in both everyday commerce and science.

Sidemount, SM: A scuba gear configuration where one, two or more cylinders are worn at the side(s) below the armpits aligned with the hips rather than on the back. Originally used in cave diving but now popular in several other applications.

Silt-out: Loss of visibility at depth due to diver's actions disturbing sediment. Particularly dangerous in an overhead environment such as a cave or wreck.

Six Skills, The: Term originally coined in diving by Steve Lewis as a teaching aid and used to catalog the essential components of physical and mental skills contributing to safe diving: Buoyancy, Trim, Movement & Position, Breathing, Situational Awareness, and Emotional Control.

Snoopy Loop: A home-made heavy-duty elastic band made from a slice of bicycle, trailer or car tire inner tube.

Soda Lime: Depreciated term in diving which describes the mixture of chemicals, used in granular form in rebreathers, recompression chambers, submarines and operating theatres to remove carbon dioxide from breathing gases to prevent CO2 retention and carbon dioxide poisoning. The principal ingredients of soda lime are calcium hydroxide, water, sodium hydroxide, and potassium hydroxide.

S-Drill: Part of pre-dive buddy/team checks includes going through simulated OOA donation with buddy or buddies.

Sofnolime: A popular brand of soda lime manufactured by Molecular Products Group Worldwide. Sofnolime is a trademark of Molecular but is close to becoming the generic name used to describe all scrubber materials used in rebreather diving.

SOP, SOPs: Standing (or Standard) Operating Procedures: Detailed documentation to describe the selection of personnel, equipment and best practices for goal-oriented underwater tasks.

SPG: Submersible Pressure Gauge, in technical and advanced diving is a small (usually 5-8 cm / 2-21/2-inch diameter) brass cased gauge not encased in a console or rubber mount. It may read tank pressure in BAR or PSI.

Spool: Small device for storing and deploying cave line, usually nylon, plastic or delrin but also metal. No moving parts, small, compact, economical and reliable alternative to a reel for relatively short lines.

Sport diving: A form of recreational scuba diving conducted within No Decompression Limits (NDL) and done in open water (non-overhead) environment only.

Survival Techniques: Formal name for the accident protection guidelines developed from Sheck Exley's original ideas published in *Blueprint for Survival*. These are Attitude; Knowledge; Training; Gas Supply; Gas Mix; Exposure; Equipment; and Operations.

T

Tank: Popular slang term used to describe a high-pressure scuba cylinder.

Technical Diver's Credo: Any diver can call any dive at any time for any reason without fear of reproach. Also known as The Golden Rule. A catch-phrase to underscore the most basic of risk-management tactics: if it doesn't feel right, bailout!

Technical Diving: A phrase coined by author and magazine publisher Michael Menduno in the early 1990 to describe the activities of a small group of recreational divers who were conducting deep, staged decompression dives.

Technical Diving International, TDI: The largest technical diving certification agency in the world, and one of the first agencies to offer mixed gas and rebreather training.

Thumb a dive: Abort or cancel a dive immediately and without question. From the diver's Thumbs Up signal meaning "Surface Now!"

Traditional North Florida Cave Diver's Rig: Hogarthian-style back plate, wing, long hose, bungeed necklace.

Trimix: A blend of oxygen, helium and nitrogen to produce a breathing mixture taking advantage of helium's characteristics to manage inert-gas narcosis and CNS oxygen toxicity. Trimix is labelled with oxygen percentage first, helium second and very rarely lists nitrogen content at all. For example an 18/45 trimix would contain 18 percent oxygen and 45 percent helium, and 37 percent nitrogen.

U

Unicorn Scenario: Unrealistic suggestion or speculation.

V

V-Planner: Is a decompression program that uses the Varying Permeability Model (VPM-B) for decompression profiles. Written by Ross Hemingway (developer of the 2ZPlanner program) when he adapted the VPM Fortran codes produced by Erik Baker from its DOS console state, into a full Windows program. This was the first Windows program with VPM, and the general public had its first look at the new program, released as a freeware, in July 2001.

VPM: Varying Permeability Model VPM-B decompression model is well suited to today's technical diving. The dive profile from a VPM-B profile is a one that includes both deep stops and modest amount of time in the shallow areas. The basic concept of a bubble model is to limit and control bubble growth and bubble sizes to smaller amounts through the ascent, thereby avoiding the damaging effects of any larger bubbles.

W

Wet Breathe: To test a regulator second stage function by immersing it in water and breathing from it. Considered a better pre-dive test than breathing in air since wet breathing will show tendencies of regulator to allow water to leak into diver's mouth.

WOB, Work of Breathing: The effort expended in inhaling and exhaling the breathing gas.

X

X, Brand: Term used to tag a generic product or service.

X-Ray Magazine: Is the highest ranked onLine international scuba diving periodical publishing articles on diving destinations, techniques, news and equipment of a truly global nature and found at xray-mag.com

Y

Yoke Adaptor: A device used to connect a regulator or filling whip with a DIN thread to an international connection cylinder valve.

Y-Valve: A cylinder valve with two outlets and two hand wheels that can be independently controlled allowing two regulator first stages to be used for some level of redundancy. Similar to H-valve but in Y configuration. Also known as Slingshot valve.

Yount, David: Primarily remembered for his work with David Hoffman and others to develop VPM and suggest it for use in professional diving and recreational diving. Collaborated with Eric B. Maiken, and Erik C. Baker between 1999 and 2000 to apply the VPM decompression algorithm to model repetitive, mixed-gas decompression diving.

Z

ZIP Code: Is the system of postal codes used by the United States Postal Service since the 1960s. Although a ZIP code does not designate a geographic area, to say that something or someone is "in the same ZIP code," means they are close by.

Zip Tie: Self-locking plastic strip used to "tie" or secure things such as a bolt snap to a dive light. Convenient to use but prone to breaking at the most inopportune times especially in cold conditions.

ZHL-16, ZHL-8 Bühlmann decompression algorithm: are two mathematical models based on the dissolved gas decompression model derived and tested by Dr. A. Bühlmann in Zurich, Switzerland beginning in 1959 with his findings first published in 1983.

ABOUT THE AUTHOR

Steve Lewis has been an active technical diver, instructor and expedition leader since the early 1990s when diving was an antidote to a career in marketing and brand management. In 2002 he left the corporate world and became a dive bum full-time, and is currently a training, marketing and communications consultant in the diving industry for clients in the public and private sectors.

His other professional credits include serving on the Training Advisory Panel for TDI, SDI, ERDI, working as managing editor for Diving Adventure Magazine, and as a contributing editor for Underwater Journal. He is also a regular contributor of articles and essays for several onLine publications including X-Ray Magazine. Steve has authored and co-authored several diving textbooks including the best-selling *Six Skills and Other Discussions.*

He has a home shared with his wife, their pets, an array of garden implements and snow removal equipment very near the eastern shore of Georgian Bay – part of Lake Huron – in Muskoka, Ontario. When not hidden away among the boreal forests of Canada's Lakelands, he travels extensively to deliver diver and instructor training programs across North America and the Caribbean, Europe and Asia.

As a speaker, educator, and blogger, he is best known for promoting safe diving practices to recreational divers who plan to use both open and closed-circuit kit, in caves, on wrecks and in open water environments.

An optimist at heart, he hopes one day, to see Millwall win the FA Cup.

Made in the USA
San Bernardino, CA
17 December 2015